Charles
Redd
Monographs
in Western
History No. 12

THE
TWENTIETH CENTURY
American West

CONTRIBUTIONS TO AN UNDERSTANDING

Thomas G. Alexander and
John F. Bluth
Editors

Charles Redd Center for Western Studies

The Charles Redd Monographs in Western History are made possible by a grant from Charles Redd. This grant served as the basis for the establishment of the Charles Redd Center for Western Studies at Brigham Young University.

Center editors: Thomas G. Alexander
Howard A. Christy
Phyllis Colonna

ISBN   0-941214-09-5

Charles Redd Center for Western Studies
© 1983 by Charles Redd for Western Studies. All rights reserved
Printed in the United States of America

Distributed by Signature Books, Midvale, Utah

Contents

Introduction   *Thomas G. Alexander*   vii

Mirror for the Future: the Historical Past
of the Twentieth-Century West   *Gerald D. Nash*   1

Coal Mining in the Rocky Mountains:
Boom, Bust, and Boom   *H. Lee Scamehorn*   29

The Transformation of Utah's
Agriculture, 1847-1900   *Davis Bitton and Linda Wilcox*   57

Young Heber J. Grant:
Enterprenuer Extraordinary   *Ronald W. Walker*   85

Introduction

In order to understand the American West today, it is essential that we analyze those features that have persisted from the nineteenth century. As Gerald Nash writes in the essay opening this volume, such analysis is often difficult because we imagine the nineteenth-century West to be filled with cowboys, Indians, sourdough miners, and other so-called frontier types. The reality, however, is somewhat different. More typical were the farmers, businessmen, laborers, corporations, governmental officials, and minority groups who still people the region today.

The American West did not end in 1890. Although significant changes have evolved, such changes as have taken place have come from previous conditions; there have been no sudden appearance of discontinuous patterns. In an attempt to provide evidence of the continuity that has been obtained, the following four essays, lectures previously given in a series sponsored by the Charles Redd Center for Western Studies, are presented. The essays by Gerald D. Nash and by H. Lee Scamehorn focus directly on the twentieth century while the two essays by Davis Bitton and Linda Wilcox and Ronald W. Walker focus on trends that began in the nineteenth century and that have continued into the twentieth century.

The two twentieth-century essays examine their subjects from a broad point of view. Focusing primarily on economic change, but also looking at ethnic patterns, Nash rejects the myth of the closing frontier and examines the continuities between the nineteenth and twentieth centuries. Scamehorn examines the coal-mining industry, increasingly important as the United States has come to rely more on fossil fuels.

Although both essays recognize the changes that have taken place over time, a significant feature of both is their emphasis on continuity. As in the nineteenth century, extractive industries continue to play an important role in the Western economy. Manufacturing tends to lag behind the rest of the nation, while postindustrial service industries tend to provide a larger employment than in the remainder of the United States. Even minority-group problems, extensive in the nineteenth-century West, continue as a significant feature today.

The other two essays are more narrowly focused. Davis Bitton and Linda Wilcox interpret the reasons for change and development in agriculture in late nineteenth-century Utah. The introduction of new plant strains and improved farm machinery led Utah along a path of change not unlike that followed by other states. A significant difference, and one that made Utah uniquely Western, was in the development of better irrigation techniques. Beyond this, the promotional activities of the Mormon church made Utah less like other states, even those in the West.

Ronald W. Walker's essay considers the business activities of a single individual—Heber J. Grant. An entrepreneur of the classical Victorian type, his career was undoubtedly similar to that of hundreds of other businessmen in the late nineteenth-century United States. The major difference was in his ecclesiastical position. Even here, however, his devotion to religious ideals would not have distinguished him from such other entrepreneurs as John D. Rockefeller.

These essays will be found useful as an addition to the growing body of evidence showing the continuity between the nineteenth- and twentieth-century West. The West persists and changes, and new patterns evolve from the old. In light of currently available evidence, it seems unlikely that we can look at the nineteenth century as an isolated and discontinuous phenomenon except in a symbolic and mythical sense. It is rather to be seen as carrying the twentieth century in embryo.

Mirror for the Future:
The Historical Past of the
Twentieth-Century West

Gerald D. Nash

In this introductory essay, Gerald D. Nash, Professor of
History at the University of New Mexico, looks at the broad
sweep of Western development as well as problems in the
twentieth century. He suggests that to understand the West
today we must understand the West since 1890. We may well
have insisted on too much discontinuity with the alleged closing
of the frontier in 1890, thus failing to realize that the same sort
of concerns—in a somewhat different form perhaps—are
present today.

He focuses essentially on two problems: the need for natural
resources, and the difficulties of minority acculturation. As in
the nineteenth century, Westerners today are concerned about
resource use. Then it was land and water; today the scope has
broadened to include fossil fuels, tourism, and space for
scientific endeavors. In the nineteenth century, the acculturation of Indians and Chinese gave Westerners much to consider.
Today the Indian has remained, but the Hispanic-American has
replaced the Chinese as the second principal unassimilated
minority group.

It seems clear, however, that these problems are much more
complex today than in the last century or even in the 1930s and
40s. Today we insist upon a relatively clean environment. The
defense installations that were viewed as the saviors of many

Western states during World War II are now suspect. Take for example the massive opposition to the MX missile-basing system. We wonder today whether what seemed a rather liberal Native American policy in the 1930s might not be cultural imperialism in a form that substitutes political democracy for yeoman agriculture. Many Westerners are concerned about the colonialism of the federal government as well as the colonialism of private corporations. These problems must be solved, but if they are addressed, as Professor Nash suggests, it will only be through a better understanding of the meaning of the West in the twentieth century.

In a rapidly growing region such as the twentieth-century West, it has often seemed that rapid expansion spawned a bevy of new problems for each generation. Yet historians know that first appearances can be illusory. Many of the issues that engage the attention of Westerners today are not novel. Rather these problems have deep roots in the region's historical past. Continuity as much as change has been a central theme of Western development since 1890, and if we are to understand some of the major problems of the twentieth-century West, we must approach them in their historical context. These problems grew out of a complicated web of past experience, and in that sense the past provides a mirror for the future.

Much of the history of the twentieth-century West is still unclear. Hence the patterns that have characterized its growth are obscure. This generation of Westerners has the task of discerning those patterns. At this stage of research any such analysis must be highly tentative, but the effort should be made. This essay touches upon selected patterns of historical growth as they bear on major issues the region faces in the last quarter of the twentieth century. These include the following: patterns of self-image, patterns of resource exploitation, patterns of economic growth, and patterns of acculturation of minorities.

In the absence of detailed knowledge, our perceptions of these problems are often clouded or distorted. The effort to clarify them will require the work of not one but many scholars.[1]

It is perhaps a truism that the image most Americans have of the West since 1890 is blurred. This blurred image of the New West is in stark contrast to the image of the Old West that is held in the American mind. That image comes in loud and clear. It brings to mind cowboys and Indians, boom towns and outlaws, and a sense of freedom and excitement.[2] But to conjure up an image of the West since 1890 is far more difficult. That diffuse image may include California surfing and split-level houses, the Arizona desert, the great Mormon temple in Salt Lake City, the vast cattle ranges of Wyoming, or the mist-shrouded forests of the Northwest. Even Westerners themselves have only a dim vision of the unique or distinctive features of their region. The patterns of development that characterized its growth in the twentieth century are still largely underdeveloped and unclear.[3] And yet, people who are unclear about their past have greater difficulty in planning for their future than those whose sense of identity is more firmly fixed.

The reasons for the ambivalence that hovers over the image of the twentieth-century West are not difficult to find. The extraordinary rapidity of growth in the twentieth century tended to crush prevailing historical traditions. The influx of more than 40 million newcomers into the trans-Mississippi West between 1890 and 1970 brought a veritable mélange—a tremendous mixing of peoples with differing cultural traditions—into the region. And the waves of newcomers came in such rapid succession that before 1970 insufficient time had elapsed to allow a distinctive cultural amalgam. Moreover, throughout the twentieth century nationalizing influences in American life, partly through the mass media, seemed to submerge regional or local peculiarities.

But to some extent the failure of Westerners in the twentieth century to develop a clear sense of regional distinctiveness was due to the persistence of a myth about the place of the West in national life after 1890. Most Westerners—like most Americans—assumed that after 1890 the West ceased to exist. With the assumed closing of the frontier, the golden age of the West supposedly came to an end. Whatever happened thereafter was an anticlimax—the pallid reflection, at best, of the exciting and stirring events of frontier life. This self-deprecating image has, I believe, played an important role in hindering the formulation of a clearly held sense of Western identity in the twentieth century.

I would argue, however, that such a concept has been rooted in myth rather than in fact. For the twentieth century witnessed perhaps the most dramatic and significant period in Western history to date. It deserves to be explored and documented in its own right and to be looked upon by Westerners with pride and admiration.

Certainly the myth that the West entered a new era in 1890 needs to be explored—and exploded—as a first step in the development of what we can hope will be a more clearly defined sense of regional identity in the future. Let me analyze one segment of the myth to demonstrate how it may have blocked an awareness of the distinction of the twentieth-century West.

In 1893 Americans were told by no less an authority than Frederick Jackson Turner that the frontier had ceased to exist in 1890. During succeeding decades this declaration was often accepted at face value by the general public as well as by a wide range of scholars.[4] Let us explore this assumption further.

It is indeed ironic that this myth was in part propounded by one of the most often quoted but least known individuals in nineteenth-century America: Robert P. Porter. Who was Robert P. Porter? His name does not appear in contemporary writings, it is strangely absent from history books about the West, and we look in vain for mention of it in the learned journals or rosters of professional societies. Even the extensive biography of Frederick Jackson Turner by Ray A. Billington neglects all mention of him. Porter was an obscure government bureaucrat, the U. S. Superintendent of the Census between 1889 and 1893. It was he who wrote the now famous report on the U. S. Census of 1890 in which he declared that the frontier was gone and that a significant epoch in the American experience had just ended. He declared:

> Up to and including 1880 the country had a frontier of settlement, but at present the unsettled area has been so broken into by isolated bodies of settlement that there can hardly be said to be a frontier line. In the discussion of its extent, its westward

movement etc., it cannot, therefore, any longer have a place in the census reports.[5]

Those were the phrases that were to launch a new national mood. They led Frederick Jackson Turner to write his famous essay on "The Significance of the Frontier in American History." There, on the first page, Turner approvingly quoted the anonymous superintendent of the census to provide justification for his own argument, thus giving rise to a new school of American history and thought. Little did Porter realize the dimensions of the new movement of which, inadvertently, he was a founder.

That the propagator of one of the most enduring myths in the American mind should also be one of the least known figures in our history is indeed a paradox. Porter was born in Norwich, England, on 30 June 1852. He came to the United States in his youth and in 1872 began a journalistic career on the Chicago *Inter-Ocean*. An active Republican, he was first retained as an adviser to the U. S. Census in 1880 and 1881, reporting on wealth and the impact of taxation. He made similar reports for the newly established U. S. Tariff Commission in 1882 before moving to New York City, where, from 1884 to 1887, he served on the editorial staff of the New York *Tribune*. In 1889 his political connections attracted the attention of President Benjamin Harrison, who appointed him Superintendent of the Eleventh U. S. Census, a post he held for four years. With the advent of Grover Cleveland and the Democrats in 1893, he returned to private life. But in 1898 President William McKinley appointed him as a special fiscal and tariff commissioner to Cuba. Upon completion of these duties Porter returned to England where he became a member of the staff of the *London Times* and where he remained until his death in 1917. In addition to his newspaper articles he wrote various books, including *The Free Trade Folly*, *The Life of William McKinley*, *The Dangers of Municipal Ownership*, *The Full Recognition of Japan*, and *The Ten Republics*.[6] Clearly, Porter was a prolific journalist who wrote on a great variety of topics, but he could hardly be considered an expert on demography or population.

Since he was not a specialist on census data, the findings of the U. S. Census Office in 1890 should not be accepted without critical appraisal. In actuality historians have yet to explore the workings of the Census Office and its operation in any detail. Until 1895 the federal government had no regular census office; every ten years a temporary staff was gathered into a skeleton organization that ceased its existence after the initial compilation of information. The task of confronting the sometimes inexperienced political appointees who served as Superintendent of the Census was enormous. Porter himself described his tribulations before an investigatory committee of the House of Representatives in 1894.

> When I was appointed I had nothing but one clerk and a messenger, and a desk with some white paper in it. . . . Then the difficulty comes in getting your force together, picking out your men. I was not able to get more than three of the old men from this city. . . . Then, knowing all the old special agents of the Tenth Census I wrote asking them if they were prepared to take up the work again. Some were and some declined. . . . Some were dead and some in private business. I succeeded getting one from Colorado. . . . He had a good practice out there as a lawyer in Denver, where he had gone originally for his health. I could not pay him as much as he was making, but he was fond of statistical work and was desirous of again taking up the inquiry he had conducted in the Tenth Census. With these men we started up the organization.

Porter went on to describe difficulties due to lack of a permanent organization. He had to devise anew many of the forms and questionnaires needed to gather necessary information. Yet, he lamented,

> to guide us in setting up these blanks we had only a few scrapbooks that someone had had the forethought to use in saving some of the forms of blanks in the last census. We had taken them home, a few copies at a time, and put them into scrapbooks. The Government had taken no care of these things in 1885, when the office was closed up. Some of them had been sold for waste paper, others have been burned, and others lost.[7]

Clearly, the Census of 1890 was not a highly professional organization.

In fact, the operations of the census office in 1890 came in for severe criticism by contemporaries. Since Porter hired more than twenty-five hundred employees for the task, his policies came under the close scrutiny of the U. S. Civil Service Commission, headed by none other than young Theodore Roosevelt. The future president was concerned about the qualifications of census office employees and particularly irritated by Porter's reluctance to enforce civil service rules in his agency. Roosevelt, as well as the congressional investigators in the House, raised serious questions about the professional competence of many census workers. True, Porter was trying his best under difficult conditions. Moreover, he had been able to attract some able individuals.[8] On the other hand, the accuracy of many of the reports—particularly those dealing with demographic data—was by no means absolute. Thus, the assertion that the frontier had disappeared in 1890 was impressionistic, a reflection of Porter's journalistic style rather than a generalization that flowed from the accumulation of census data. Many areas of the West continued to have a population of fewer than two-to-six persons per square mile. Whether significant changes occurred in population density in 1890 as compared to 1880, 1900, or 1910 is open to question. What is certain, however, is that the assumptions, the methods, and the conclusions of the Census of 1890 need to be carefully weighed and evaluated.[9]

And so the myths of one century, the nineteenth, gave way to another, the twentieth. The myth of the Old West gave way to the myth that after 1890 there was in fact no frontier—no West that was distinctively different from other parts of the nation. This myth remained firmly entrenched in the minds of millions of Americans, pervading books, articles, motion pictures, and other materials out of which myths are made. Symbolically, of course, the late nineteenth century witnessed major changes in American life, particularly the transformation of an agrarian society into an industrial civilization. In that process Western agriculture and Western lands lost their erstwhile primacy in national life, but the West itself underwent no startling changes in 1890. In the course of the ensuing eighty years it embarked, however, upon the most rapid growth in its entire history.

The significance of this growth rarely intruded upon the self-image of Westerners. Most writings about the West, whether in literature, history, or folklore, have concentrated on the Old West. If the bulk of written material is an index of its importance, the West after 1890 constituted a veritable desert, not apparently worthy of consideration. Certainly it is difficult to plan for the West in the future without a clear sense of growth patterns of the past. One of the most pressing needs in studies concerning the twentieth-century West, therefore, is the formulation of a clearer sense of self-image for the region.

In the last quarter of the twentieth century, long-dormant problems of environmental balance have emerged in the consciousness of Westerners. Since portions of the region, particularly the Sunbelt states, are experiencing a veritable boom in the 1970s and 1980s, their rapid growth adds urgency to the prospects of depletion and pollution in the immediate future. Historical perspective may provide guidance in dealing with these problems.

One concern of Westerners in the twentieth and twenty-first centuries must of necessity be cycles in the weather patterns of the region. Climatologists have recorded alternating cycles of dry and wet weather for the West over hundreds of years and have reconstructed charts that trace the cycles over thousands of years. These climatic changes provide a context within which to evaluate man-made or cultural forces. The reasons for climatic cycles are well known and include earth reactions to solar and volcanic changes. Moreover, gravitational pulls of orbiting planets, such as Jupiter, are a factor; they affect the tides that exert stresses on the earth's thin crust, ultimately influencing dry and humid climates. Such silent changes also subtly affect cultural or man-made conditions.

In 1976 some climatologists announced their belief that the West has embarked on a long period of drought. For example, between 1970 and 1976 the Dakotas, Kansas, and California experienced severe droughts and increasingly erratic weather patterns. According to one expert, Dr. Iben Browning, the West has moved into a highly unpredictable, erratic pattern characterized by a cooling trend that will severely affect agricultural production, economic stability, and social order. During such periods the average line of good climate and favorable growing conditions in the northern hemisphere shifts southwards. In the United States this average line runs roughly across the center of the nation on an east-west axis; the states north of this line are likely to become colder and drier during the next hundred years, and agricultural production is likely to shift further southward. It is not accidental therefore that the fastest growing portion of the West in 1976 is found in the Sunbelt states, situated on the southern rim of the shifting climate line. And, predicts Dr. Browning,

> regional friction is going to increase enormously. People in states producing raw products like food, fiber, and fuel are no longer little people as they used to be when people in cities were in power. They've got muscle of their own now, and they see cash markets in the rest of the world. There is no special virtue a Kansas wheat farmer can see in feeding a New Yorker over feeding a Russian— especially if the Russian pays.[10]

The implications of current climatological predictions are clear. Shifting climatic patterns in the late twentieth century are likely to result in a cooling cycle that will characterize another period of erratic weather patterns. Such patterns could readily introduce another era of unsettled mobility in the West not unlike the decade of the 1930s. Moreover, the cooling cycle may affect western states north of the 41st parallel with special adversity and at the same time lead to a shift of population, wealth, and productivity to western states south of the 41st parallel. This process may already be underway, for by 1970 various writers began to call attention to the extraordinarily rapid growth spurt in the Sunbelt states—running in an arc-like tier from Georgia westward through Louisiana, Texas, the Southwest, and California. This region was making phenomenal strides in population growth, accumulation of wealth, and productivity. Once one of the nation's most under-developed areas, by 1970 it was America's newest boomtown frontier. The historical pattern of weather changes in the West, therefore, presents future planners with serious issues.

Not only climate but also resource depletion has emerged as

a major environmental issue for the West in the last quarter of the twentieth century, and the historical experience of western resource development may be instructive in reflecting upon resource policies of the future.

That the record of western resource exploitation since the nineteenth century is one of maximum depletion is well known. Such a trend has been the result of prevailing American values, often based on the assumption that the nation's store of natural resources was virtually unlimited. Perhaps the post-Civil War generation was the first to question the myth of limitless resources as people became aware of the pressure of increasing population on existing known raw materials. As a result, the states and the national government established investigatory commissions between 1875 and 1890 that did pioneer work in making accurate surveys. In the ensuing decade public interest in conservation flagged as the economic depression of the 1890s became a major national concern. During the Progressive Era, however, another wave of conservation consciousness swept the nation. It culminated between 1905 and 1915 in the adoption of limited regulatory policies by the states, the federal government, and some large corporations. World War I dampened the ardor of conservationist groups, but by the 1930s the Great Depression reawakened public consciousness about the nation's shrinking stock of natural resources. It led to the establishment of positive government conservation programs and an increase of federal and state regulatory controls. Public concern with conservation waned during World War II and for two decades thereafter when technological advances appeared to expand the nation's resources virtually without limit. By the mid-1960s, however, the rapid desecration of the environment—reflected in air and water pollution as well as shortages in gas and oil—again brought Americans face to face with the specter of scarcity.[11] Once more an aroused public consciousness spawned a wide array of environmental measures by governments as well as private groups designed to preserve the environment or to allow its exploitation only under controlled conditions.

This cursory review of conservation movements reveals that

the environmental concerns of Americans have been characterized by alternating cycles. These have fluctuated between keen concern over limited resources and wastefulness and unconcern. In 1976 Americans were in the midst of another cycle of concern—at a time when the rate of depletion was greater than in any previous period. If past experience is any indication, therefore, the great interest in environmentalism of the mid-1970s will diminish within another decade unless extreme shortages should intervene. Whether the cycles of conservation and waste can be broken during the last quarter of the twentieth century remains to be seen.

Yet it would be desirable if history did not repeat itself—if the concern over environmental issues of the 1970s did not recede into oblivion to be revived only by another crisis. In fact, history does not repeat itself. The nation's store of resources at the end of the twentieth century may well be smaller in relation to its population than at any previous period; hence the need for reduction of waste is far more pressing than in previous years. Since public awareness of environmental problems has fluctuated so erratically in the past, it seems highly desirable for Americans to provide more systematic and stable management of resource development in the future. The creation of the Environmental Protection Agency appears to be a step in the right direction. But even more urgently needed are more explicit and clearly defined resource policies by government, corporations, and voluntary groups. Until 1970 American resource policies were characterized primarily by drift and indecision. Thereafter a growing awareness of impending energy shortages prompted public discussions of possible alternatives for national resources policies.

The absence of clear-cut national energy policies—and the deleterious effects—can best be illustrated by a closer analysis of one such resource, petroleum. During the first two decades of the twentieth century the federal government and the states largely abstained from interference with oil drilling and production by private interests. This period was notable for an extraordinary waste of oil and gas and for wild fluctuations in production. In some years, as in 1918 through 1920, the petroleum needs of the United States Navy were barely met. Pollution of streams in areas where oil drilling was intense came to be common. As the search for oil intensified between 1920 and 1941, oil producers found that they could not operate effectively without the aid of state and federal governments. Waste and duplication of drilling became so wanton as to threaten the price structure of the industry. Overproduction seriously disrupted markets.

In this period the industry thus did a turnabout; it came to favor government regulation of oil production, and ultimately the regulation of the entire oil industry. State pro rata laws, the Petroleum Code of the National Recovery Administration, the Connally Act, and the Interstate Oil Compact were government responses to industry demands. Yet in 1941, just before United States involvement in World War II, the nation still lacked a national petroleum policy. As war demands mounted, the federal government—under the leadership of Secretary of the Interior Harold Ickes, who directed the Petroleum Administration for War—exercised strict controls over many phases of petroleum production and marketing. Ickes was keenly aware of the need for some form of clearly developed national oil policy for the post-war era, a policy that would balance conservation with production for use. But in the industry and in Congress bitter opposition developed during 1945 and 1946 to any change in the status quo governing the relation between the industry and state and federal governments, and the effort by Ickes to formulate a national oil policy was a failure.

Between 1945 and 1970 the pattern of industry-government relations continued without significant changes. Essentially, the petroleum industry shaped state and federal policies to accord with its own particular interests and desires.[12] The results of this type of self-government became increasingly apparent during the 1960s. Widespread air pollution in large cities, particularly western cities such as Los Angeles and Denver where mountainous areas contained the noxious fumes, was one visible effect. Air pollution was greatly accentuated by the petroleum industry's shift to leaded gasolines in 1950 to supply needlessly powerful automobiles with high-consumption, high-compression engines. The oil industry's singleminded effort to promote greater gasoline consumption also led to the rapid decline of urban mass transit systems after World War II. In San Francisco during 1945 a corporation controlled by General Motors, Exxon, and the Goodyear Tire Company bought the electric trolley lines of the Bay Transit Company—then promptly replaced them with General Motors buses operating on Exxon gasoline and rolling on Goodyear Tires. Similarly, before 1945 Los Angeles had the world's largest urban electric railway network, but in 1940 a corporation controlled by General Motors, Standard Oil of California, and the Firestone Company acquired the interurban system, scrapped the rail lines, and replaced them in part with General Motors buses. Altogether, one hundred electric rail lines in forty-five cities, including New York, Philadelphia, and Salt Lake City, were abandoned.[13] Another serious result of the policy of encouraging maximum consumption by American automobile owners was to accentuate inflationary pressures in the United States. As the demand for petroleum increased, prices rose steadily. Increased dependence on petroleum products made them a larger component of the total cost-of-living index and contributed to an upward price spiral in the two decades after 1950.

At the same time an increased dependence on foreign oil supplies was reflected in a sharply increased percentage of foreign oil imports between 1950 and 1975. This certainly affected the nation's balance-of-trade deficit—and further contributed to inflation. At the same time it led the United States to increasing political involvement in the Middle East and elsewhere. Thus the absence of a clearly formulated national oil policy had a profound impact on the nation and the West.[14] It contributed to the rapid depletion of one of the West's major natural resources, it created vast areas plagued by injurious air pollution, and it became a major cause of inflationary pressures.

The historical development of other natural resources in the twentieth-century West—such as coal, copper, and uranium—pinpoints a similar trend. Between 1900 and 1970 environmental considerations were clearly subservient to profit motives. Conscious of living in an underdeveloped region, Westerners were extremely anxious to attract needed capital to exploit natural resources. Hence the historic Western pattern in mining development was characterized by a succession of booms and busts. That was the history of California gold in the 1850s, Nevada silver in the 1860s, Colorado gold and silver in the 1870s, and Montana copper in the 1940s. But the closing of Montana copper mines did not end the era of Western mining. New innovations in mining technology generated another boom. Kerr/McKee opened vast new uranium mines in New Mexico between 1950 and 1975, large coal companies such as Peabody Coal reopened mines in Utah and Colorado, the major oil companies undertook serious prospecting of oil shales in Colorado, and the Phelps-Dodge Corporation built a vast new copper-mining complex near Tyrone, New Mexico. Many of those operations resulted in further desecrating the environment.

That the West was on the verge of another major mining boom was clear by 1970. As the historical experience of Western mining should indicate, from the perspective of resource conservation it would not be desirable to repeat the patterns of boom and bust so common in the past. Each mining boom left the environment a little more denuded than before. Undoubtedly such fears generated another surge of environmental consciousness in the decade after 1965; various laws on the state and national levels, such as the Air Quality Act of 1965 and the Strip Mining Laws of 1970 and 1971, reflected a desire to provide protection for the environment and to introduce values other than the profit motive in the formulation of public policies. Since conservation issues increasingly revolved about highly specialized and technical data comprehended largely by experts, would-be developers and corporations often had an advantage over less specialized spokespersons for environmental groups.[15] Without clearly delineated policies, and without a sense of the Western experience in the twentieth century and changes wrought by the passage of time, current environmental concerns may fade as quickly as they did in previous eras.

Of course, many of the environmental problems of the modern West are intimately related to the economic development of the region, and throughout much of the twentieth century that economic growth has been characterized by a type of colonialism—economic dominance by the richer and more highly industrialized East. Much like an underdeveloped nation, the West since 1890 has been a purveyor of raw materials for the factories and mills of the East. In the process Westerners have shipped much of their wealth outside the region while retaining only modest profits. Over the years this colonial relationship has troubled many critics, none more so than the late Walter P. Webb. In 1937 he wrote one of his angriest books, *Divided We Stand*, in which he chastised the East severely for maintaining the West in economic bondage. Since that time the West has made considerable strides in its industrial development, yet the shackles of the past are not cast off easily or quickly. In the years between 1941 and 1975 colonialism had not disappeared from the relationships between the regions.

In his pathbreaking study of Western economic growth, Professor Leonard J. Arrington documented some features of colonialism. Over a period of ninety years, from 1860 to 1950, the sources of income for most Western states changed little. Exports of raw materials, tourism, and expenditures by military bases and installations provided the major sources of income for the Mountain states, California, and the Pacific rim. Professor Arrington concluded his study in 1950,[16] but in the years from 1950 to 1975 the pattern he outlined did not change significantly. Economic growth of the West between 1950 and 1975 was significantly affected by its heritage of colonialism before World War II.[17]

The economy of the twentieth-century West was also shaped to a considerable degree by environmental influences that continued to have a profound effect in the eight decades after 1890. During this period the West continued to be far behind the rest of the nation in manufacturing production. Instead it was a major producer of raw materials and, by reason of its natural environment, the home of burgeoning new space-age industries. A few examples will illustrate.

Between 1900 and 1914 Western manufacturers were only 5 percent of the national total; between the two world wars there was little change. Between 1945 and 1975 the West tried hard to catch up with the rest of the nation, but although its manufacturing growth was spectacular, it was still behind older regions. In 1970 the Western states accounted for 12 percent of the national production. If this growth trend continues in the next three decades, around the year 2020 we can expect the West to approximate the manufacturing production of other sections.

The paucity of manufacturers in the West was dramatically underscored by the absence of a steel industry. In 1941 the only steel manufacturing facility was at the Colorado Fuel and Iron Company Works in Pueblo, Colorado. Like a colony, the vast expanse west of the Mississippi River was dependent on eastern manufacturing centers for its steel. This dependence became painfully evident to Westerners with the entrance of the United States into World War II. Several Western states sent delegations to Washington, D. C., pleading for federal monies to develop this crucial industry. Of the various applicants, industrialist Henry J. Kaiser became the most successful. In 1942 he and United States Steel Corporation received more than $200 million from the Defense Plant Corporation to construct new steel fabrication facilities in Fontana, California, and Orem, Utah. In 1975 they remained the sole major steel-manufacturing centers west of the Mississippi River. Despite progress, however, the West's disadvantages for the location of heavy industries has continued to prevent extensive growth.

When Westerners did try to develop industries and manufactures, they did so by taking advantage of the particular environmental conditions of the region. Thus it is not surprising that space-age industries were spawned in the West after 1941. In part this development was a result of deliberate policies by the federal government to disperse industries relevant to national security. But Western land and space offered other incentives as well. The vast empty stretches of the West offered unusual opportunities for geographic isolation and secrecy, and the rapidly growing but dispersed cities of the region provided facilities and services necessary for the operation of large-scale technologically oriented industries. Moreover, vast spaces provided the needed testing grounds for technically sophisticated products. The favorable climates and innumerable scenic areas also provided an important magnet. Between 1945 and 1960 the federal government awarded more than 60 percent of all aerospace contracts to the West; California received 40 percent. Between 1960 and 1975 Texas succeeded California as the state that benefitted most from federal largesse in this sphere. Missile development became a major new Western enterprise. Representatives of North American Aviation, Boeing, and Hughes Aircraft stalked the West in search of new sites much as primitive fur traders had done three centuries before. Aerospace industries were particularly well geared to the West's environmental conditions.

Availability of land and space also prompted a vast expansion of federal military installations between 1940 and 1970. Increasing United States participation in Pacific affairs led the federal government to seek more supply depots and military bases west of the Mississippi River. Between 1940 and 1970 Congress authorized expenditures of more than $40 billion in the Western states. In a way, construction of the United States Air Force Academy in Colorado Springs after the Second World War was symbolic of the westward movement of the American military establishment. Vandenberg Air Force Base in California and the huge federal supply depot in Ogden, Utah, were examples of the vast new network of installations that played a crucial role in bolstering the Western economy. Similarly, missile complexes such as the Minuteman missile facility in Montana or the Kennedy Space Center in Texas were built to take advantage of particular characteristics of the West.

Availability of sparsely inhabited empty spaces ideally suited for the testing of airborne weapons, rockets, or spacecraft, combined with favorable climates, drew an entire generation of scientists westward after World War II. Moreover, many scientists commented that the relatively newly settled region harbored a spirit of enterprise, a willingness to experiment, that they found invigorating and infectious. In the twentieth century the West for the first time became one of the nation's most important science centers.

It is not difficult to trace the impact of environment on the growth of Western scientific centers. The plentitude of cheap power dictated establishment of the vast federal plutonium plant in Hanford, Washington, during World War II. Remoteness and isolation led to the establishment of other science centers, such as the atomic research facility at Los Alamos, New Mexico. Moreover, the vast expanses of sparsely settled mesas within its radius permitted the testing of components that would have been difficult in most other areas.

Indeed, it could be argued that for most of the twentieth century the Western economy continued as in the nineteenth century, to be shaped by its vast reserves of natural resources. Oil and gas and a score of other minerals constituted the major riches of the region. On the Pacific Coast, lumbering provided a significant share of the total income. The Rocky Mountain states produced 90 percent of the nation's copper, 50 percent of its lead, and 80 percent of its gold and silver. These states also produced substantial quantities of some of the most important alloy metals (molybdenum, vanadium, magnesium, manganese, and tungsten), while New Mexico supplied 90 percent of national potash needs.

Perhaps oil and gas were the twentieth-century West's most glamorous minerals. The exploitation of each at different periods illustrates the main theme of this essay—that the exploitation of Western resources after 1890 continued to be a central theme of Western development. The process after 1890 was not very different from the years before. Petroleum resources were intensively explored after 1901, natural gas after 1945. Until 1970 virtually all United States oil reserves were in the West. California became the nation's leading oil producer between 1890 and 1930, then Texas between 1930 and 1970. At the same time Oklahoma, Kansas, and New Mexico also became significant producers. And by the end of the century

Arizona will join the ranks of the large oil-producing states. Natural gas, a by-product of petroleum drilling, became a valuable mineral between 1945 and 1975 when technological innovations suddenly made it one of the nation's major energy resources. By 1950 Texas had become the leading producer of natural gas. As in the nineteenth century, Westerners after 1900 continued to capitalize on their land and its natural environs to foster an increasingly important tourist industry. As an increasingly affluent society found increasing time for leisure, travel became a national pastime and the West has become America's principal playground. Of the thirty-seven national parks, twenty-seven are in the West (California and Utah have five each), and the year-around recreational opportunities of the West's mountains, seashore, and national recreation areas are unmatched. The West also offered a wide range of healthful climates. The balmy temperatures of the Pacific Coast, the dry warmth of Arizona deserts in the winter—and the taming of the extreme heat of the West by air conditioning—attracted millions of Americans as tourists, many of whom became permanent settlers. And even where nature had created isolated barren wastes, as in Nevada, technological improvements turned these into assets as well. The rise of Las Vegas, Nevada, as one of the entertainment centers of the world was to a large extent dictated by its location and climate.

A major economic issue for Westerners between 1975 and 2000 will be to lessen their colonial dependence on the East and to achieve greater self-sufficiency. In this respect the course of Southern economic growth between 1950 and 1975 may provide some examples. One possible avenue to greater self-sufficiency is greater diversification of the Western economy, particularly of manufacturing and service industries. The spectacular growth of the Sunbelt states after 1970 suggests that this process is already underway. Yet this growth cannot be unfettered as in the past but rather must be planned and blended with very real environmental concerns.

Economic issues are intimately related to social problems.

Certainly the spectacular economic (and population) growth of the West since 1890 has stimulated the emergence of social problems, particularly in the area of minority relations.

Attempts at accommodation between whites and ethnic minorities have been particularly frustrating—for all concerned. The Native American experience with such attempts has been the longest and the most painful. Since 1887 it has vacillated between extremes: between attempts at total integration—with attendant destruction of traditional Native American culture—on the one hand, and attempts to allow as much self-determination (and self-expression) as possible on the other hand. Neither approach has been successful. The fact must certainly be taken into consideration by those planning public policies toward minorities in the future.

It is striking that the alternating cycles between integration (assimilation) and self-determination (tribal autonomy) have appeared with such great regularity in the course of the last one hundred years. The Dawes Act of 1887 was based partly on the premise that Indians should be treated as white men with red skins, that they could be transformed into self-sufficient farmers by an act of Congress. The experiment envisaged by the Dawes Act was bound to fail during the next generation. By the 1920s new anthropological research revealed how shallow and superficial the assumptions of the framers of the Dawes Act had been. Thus, in the post-World War I decade, groups such as the American Indian Rights Association fostered a movement to allow Native Americans self-determination and cultural self-awareness.[18]

This movement reached its apogee during the New Deal when John S. Collier served as Commissioner of Indian Affairs from 1933 to 1945. Collier was an unabashed and enthusiastic advocate of self-determination for Indians. Under his administration the Bureau of Indian Affairs encouraged tribal self-government among various tribes and greatly encouraged Indian arts and crafts and religious ceremonials. Collier sought to abolish boarding schools for Indian children and established new Indian day schools that enabled youngsters to live at home. Collier hoped to encourage greater economic self-sufficiency (on Native American terms) among the tribes.

But despite Collier's good intentions his program for such Native American independence was only partially successful. Many tribes actually lacked a native tradition encompassing a formal political structure. In some cases tribal government was therefore virtually imposed by the Bureau of Indian Affairs with the result that some tribes, bewildered by the functions of the tribal government of others, were obliged to be "Indian" in ways they did not want to be. Native cultural activities definitely increased, but some critics charged that Indian craftsmen tended to produce what they thought whites would buy rather than develop true cultural self-expression. Indian day schools at times increased cultural conflicts for youngsters, while the level of educational training remained pitiably inadequate. And the New Deal program to reduce livestock herds, another imposition (to assist the local economy in the long run by protecting the fragile land from overgrazing), eminently rational, came into conflict with Navajo cultural mores that associated ownership of livestock herds with high social status. To sum up, self-determination—as it was applied—no more assured accommodation than did forced integration.[19]

If history did not repeat itself precisely between 1945 and 1970, federal Indian policies nevertheless took another turn in a familiar cycle. Not unlike the period from 1887 to 1940, public policy again vacillated between self-determination and integration. Under the Indian Commissioners of the 1950s the Bureau of Indian Affairs sought to remove Native Americans from reservations and settle them in large urban areas. The results of this policy were disastrous for most of the Native Americans involved since they were unprepared for big city life. Tens of thousands were broken in body and in spirit while hopelessness engulfed those who remained on the reservations. It was from such experiences that a young generation of Native American leaders in the 1960s formed the Red Power movement, which placed strong emphasis on cultural awareness and self-help. New organizations such as the American Indian Movement and the National Indian Youth Council forcefully urged a return to native tribal customs and advocated racial or ethnic separatism. The majority of Native Americans did not necessarily agree with the most vocal advocates of Red Power. They were still searching for an accommodation that would allow them to retain many aspects of their culture and at the same time share in the material affluence enjoyed by the majority of Americans. One reflection of their desires was the Indian Act of 1972, which, while it returned to a policy of self-government and autonomy for Native Americans, as in the 1930s, also provided federal funds to establish industrial enterprises and industrial training on and off reservations.[20]

Since 1887, therefore, federal Indian policy has alternated between integration and separatism without finding a satisfactory accommodation. Such a historical record should provide pause for policy makers in the future. The failure of whites to comprehend the full dimension of Indian culture, their insensitivity and impatience, have all too often wrecked any chance for success. On the other hand, misunderstanding, rigidity, and a lack of realism have often characterized the Native American response to white-initiated attempts to effect true accommodation, also with detrimental results. Perhaps mutual accommodation can be pursued more successfully not only by greater patience and forebearance, but also by intensified educational training for both whites and Native Americans concerning their respective cultures. Whatever the policy, it should be formulated on the basis of past experience, which reveals that neither rapid integration nor incomplete independence has been successful in bridging the gap between the cultures.

Historical perspective may also be valuable in approaching acculturation problems of Chicanos. The acculturation of Spanish-speaking peoples has varied in the different sections of the West. Texas and New Mexico contained old families, tenth generation and beyond, who were acutely conscious of their Spanish-American heritage. Some were poor but others were prosperous in their communities. Many of those Spanish-Americans were well integrated in their communities and experienced few problems. But this was not true of the descendants of more recent arrivals from Mexico during the twentieth century, many from poor, peasant backgrounds. These newcomers have found integration into the mainstream of American life much more difficult. Their problems have been perhaps due more to cultural or class differences than to racial or ethnic discrimination. Many Chicanos in California, Arizona, and Texas during the second half of the twentieth century are descendants of Mexican immigrants who came in the great waves of immigration between 1900 and 1914 and during the 1920s. As many as 90 percent of the Mexican immigrants who came between 1919 and 1949 were landless peasants and unskilled laborers. It could hardly be expected that, without special skills or special education, they could rise easily in a highly urbanized technological society. The need for unskilled labor diminished in the United States after 1945. The roots of Chicano problems in the West may lie in these conflicting cultural and institutional mores rather than in simple racism or ethnic prejudice.[21] Nor was this Mexican-American experience in the twentieth century wholly unlike that of other immigrant groups. Social mobility was usually the product of three or more generations. From a historical perspective, the issues of Chicano acculturation were not entirely unique when compared with the experiences of such other immigrant groups as the Chinese, for example.

This brief survey has focused on the historical patterns that have characterized the major issues in the twentieth-century West. I have selected a few distinctive problems I feel are illustrative of my main theme—that the self-image of the West in the twentieth century is not as yet clearly defined. The West is not as sure of its recent past as of its roots in the nineteenth century. Yet I would argue that the solution of Western problems in the last quarter of the twentieth century is directly dependent on our perception of developmental patterns in the region after 1890. Without a clear sense of what we have become since 1890, we can hardly shape the direction of our future. Hence, it behooves students of the West to direct their study to the last eighty-five years, in the hope that an increased awareness of patterns of the recent past can provide an understanding of the present and more intelligent planning for the future. As I have tried to indicate, the shape of contemporary Western problems has been directly formed by the historical experiences of the past century. In that process which binds the generations one to the other, the experience of the West since 1890 provides a crucial—if as yet obscure—link. That link needs to be secured more effectively.

Notes

1. Among recent efforts to explore the West since 1890, see Gerald D. Nash, _The American West in the Twentieth Century_ (Englewood Cliffs, N. J.: Prentice-Hall, 1973); Howard R. Lamar, "Persistent Frontier: The West in the Twentieth Century," _Western Historical Quarterly_ 4 (1973): 5-25; John W. Caughley, "The Insignificance of the Frontier in American History or Once Upon a Time There Was an American West," _Western Historical Quarterly_ 5 (1974): 5-16; Mary Ellen Glass, "Nevada in Perspective: Some Questions for Local Historians," _Nevada Historical Quarterly_ 17 (1974): 104-8.

2. On images held by Americans concerning the West, see Henry Nash Smith, _Virgin Land: The American West as Symbol and Myth_ (Cambridge: Harvard University Press, 1950); Roderick Nash, _Wilderness and the American Mind_ (New Haven, Conn.: Yale University Press, 1967); Arthur E. Ekirch, Jr., _Man and Nature in America_ (New York: Columbia University Press, 1963); Hans Huth, _Nature and the American: Three Centuries of Changing Attitudes_ (Berkeley: University of California Press, 1957); Mary Young, "The West and American Cultural Identity: Old Themes and New Variations," _Western Historical Quarterly_ 1 (1970): 137-60.

3. Where historians have feared to tread, journalists have not been afraid to enter. See, for example, Neal R. Pierce, _The Pacific States of America_ (New York: Norton and Co., 1972).

4. Frederick J. Turner, _The Frontier in American History_ (New York: Henry Holt and Co., 1920), p. 1.

5. U. S., Superintendent of the Census, *Report on the Population of the U. S., 1890* (Washington, D. C.: U. S. Government Printing Office, 1895), pt. 1, p. 34.

6. *Who Was Who in America, 1897-1942* (Chicago: A. N. Marquis and Co., 1943), vol. 1, p. 984. See also Robert P. Porter, *Address . . . Before the Commercial Club of St. Louis,* 21 November 1891, n.p.; "Eleventh Census," *American Statistical Association Publications* 2 (September 1891): 321-79; and "Eleventh Census," *Journal of the Royal Statistical Society* 57 (December 1894): 643-77. For Porter's service as Superintendent of the Eleventh U. S. Census, see U. S., National Archives, *Preliminary Inventory of the Records of the Bureau of the Census,* no. 161 (Washington, D. C.: U. S. Government Printing Office, 1964), pp. 32-41.

7. U. S., Congress, House, Select Committee on a Proposal to Establish a Permanent Census Bureau, *Hearings on Operation of the Census,* 52nd Cong., 2d sess., 1892, H. Rept. 2393, quoted in W. Stull Holt, *The Bureau of the Census* (Washington, D. C.: Institute for Government Research, 1929), p. 27. See also U. S., Congress, House, *Report on the U. S. Census,* 52nd Cong., 1st sess., 1892, H. Rept. 1933, which contains extensive testimony on the workings of the Eleventh Census by its employees; and U. S., Congress, House, *Investigation of the Census,* 52nd Cong., 2d sess., 1893, H. Rept. 2617, which contains conclusions of congressional investigators.

8. U. S. Congress, House, *Review of the Census Office,* 51st Cong., 2nd sess., H. Rept. 4038, pp. 4-5, 112-30, 141-65; U. S., Congress, Senate, *Report of Examination and Review of the Census Office,* 52nd Cong., 1st sess., S. Doc. 69, 1892, pp. 26-30.

9. Personnel of the Census are listed in U. S., Superintendent of the Census, *Report, 1 December 1891,* 52nd Cong., 1st sess., S. Doc. 1. Contemporary evaluations include Francis A. Walker, "The Eleventh Census of the United States," *Quarterly Journal of Economics* 2 (January 1888): 135. Methods of the 1890 census were analyzed by a group of contemporary economists in "The Federal Census," *American Economic Association, Publications,* N.S. 2 (Princeton, 1890).

10. Iben Browning and Nels Winkless, *Climate and the Affairs of Men* (New York: Harper's Magazine Press, 1975); quotation from Browning in *New York Times,* 12 July 1976; interview with Browning,

19 February 1977, Albuquerque, N. M. For discussion of the population boom in the South and West since 1970, see *New York Times*, 12 December 1975, and 23 January, 8 February, and 14 March 1976.

11. On the conservation movement, see Douglas H. Strong, *The Conservationists* (Menlo Park, Calif.: Addison-Wesley, 1971); David Cushman Coyle, *Conservation: An American Story of Conflict and Accomplishment* (New Brunswick, N. J.: Rutgers University Press, 1957); and Gordon B. Dodds, "The Historiography of American Conservation: Past and Present," *Pacific Northwest Quarterly* 56 (1965): 75-81.

12. These developments are discussed in greater detail in Gerald D. Nash, *U. S. Oil Policy, 1890-1964* (Pittsburgh: University of Pittsburgh Press, 1968).

13. U. S., Congress, Senate, Committee on the Judiciary, Subcommittee on Antitrust and Monopoly, *American Ground Transportation*, a report by Bradford C. Snell (Washington, D. C.; U. S. Government Printing Office, 1974), pp. 30-35. See also Carl Solberg, *Oil Power: The Rise and Fall of an American Empire* (New York: New American Library, 1976), pp. 144-46.

14. From the vast literature that has appeared in recent years, see Joe Stork, *Middle East Oil and the Energy Crisis* (New York: Monthly Review Press, 1975), and E. Anthony Copp, *Regulating Competition in Oil: Government Intervention in the U. S. Refining Industry, 1948-75* (College Station: Texas A and M Press, 1976).

15. Richard H. K. Vietor, "Environmental Politics of the Coal Industry" (Ph.D. diss., University of Pittsburgh, 1975); on Tyrone, N. M., see *New York Times*, 12 October 1966; on oil shales, ibid.; and on uranium boom, ibid., 30 January 1975.

16. Leonard J. Arrington, *Changing Economic Structure of the Mountain West 1850-1950*, monograph series, vol. 10, no. 3 (Logan: Utah State University Press, 1963).

17. Nash, *American West in the Twentieth Century*; Gene Gressley, "Colonialism: A Western Complaint," *Pacific Northwest Quarterly* 54 (1963): 1-8; Neil B. Morgan, *Westward Tilt: The American West Today* (New York: Random House, 1963); Neil R.

Pierce, *The Mountain States of America* (New York: Norton and Co., 1972); idem., *The Great Plains States of America* (New York: Norton and Co., 1973).

18. With respect to one major tribe in the West, see Lawrence C. Kelly, *The Navajo Indians and Federal Indian Policy, 1900-1935* (Tucson: University of Arizona Press, 1968).

19. Donald J. Parman, *The Navajos and the New Deal* (New Haven: Yale University Press, 1976).

20. A short summary is in Stan Steiner, *The New Indians* (New York: Harper and Row, 1968).

21. A broad survey of the Chicano experience is found in Matt S. Meier and Feliciano Rivera, *The Chicanos: A History of Mexican-Americans* (New York: Hill and Wang, 1972).

Coal Mining in the Rocky Mountains: Boom, Bust, and Boom

H. Lee Scamehorn

Following a pattern noted earlier, H. Lee Scamehorn, Professor of History at the University of Colorado, points out that, from low production in the nineteenth century, the entire Intermountain West experienced a coal-mining boom during the first two decades of the twentieth century, then declining production during the 1920s and 1930s. Beginning about 1960, however, production and use increased considerably.

At the same time, the markets for the West's coal resources have changed. In the nineteenth century, principal consumers of coal were railroads, industries, and households. Since 1960, electric utilities and steelmakers have become the coal companies' major customers. The development of massive electric power plants and of strip mining mark the most significant departure from earlier patterns.

As with much in the rapidly growing West, problems have plagued recent coal development. The desire for an improved environment has brought a number of proposed coal-fired electric plants into question, resulting in the adoption of a public policy that—seemingly against all logic—forces plants burning low-sulphur Western coal to make their smoke purer than utilities burning the dirtier eastern fuel.

In the future, if petroleum supplies remain vulnerable to control by cartels like OPEC, and if major new sources of oil are not found, it seems probable that Western coal reserves will become increasingly more valuable. The impact of the exploitation of these reserves on the people of the West will be enormous, and the management of that impact will require careful consideration and wisdom.

Coal mining in the Intermountain West experienced two periods of rapid development. The first, from about 1880 to 1910, coincided with the main thrust of settlement and industrialization in the region. The era of prosperity was followed by five decades of stagnation except for brief surges during the two world wars. The second cycle began in 1960, and in recent years output has exceeded the peak levels of the earlier boom. In part, this growth is a response to the energy crisis of the 1970s and the necessity of substituting coal for dwindling supplies of petroleum and natural gas.

Historically, coal was found in abundance in most of the states of the Rocky Mountain region. Colorado, Montana, New Mexico, Utah, and Wyoming contained the solid fuel in quantity and quality to justify large-scale commercial extraction. Arizona's sizable reserves were unknown until after the turn of the century. Idaho had only minor deposits, and Nevada was without coal resources.[1]

The intermountain region possessed different grades, or varieties, of coal. Producing fields, identified by the character of their products, yielded anthracite, bituminous and subbituminous coal, and lignite. Anthracite was mined only in Gunnison County, Colorado, and Santa Fe County, New Mexico,[2] but other grades were readily accessible in many places. The principal deposits were in the Northern Plains region of Montana, with extensions into the Dakotas; the Powder River, Big Horn, and Green basins, mainly in Wyoming, with some projections into adjacent states; the Uinta Basin of eastern Utah and western Colorado; the Raton Mesa and San Juan basins of southern Colorado and northern New Mexico; and, as revealed at a later date, the Black Mesa Basin of northeastern Arizona.[3]

Coal mining in the Rocky Mountain fields grew apace with economic development in the region. Between 1880 and 1910, output increased from less than one million to more than 28 million tons, and the West's share of the nation's production rose from about 1 to 6.82 percent. The principal coal-yielding states or territories were Colorado and Wyoming, which in 1910 ranked eighth and ninth, respectively, among the twenty-six coal-producing states and territories of the United States. Montana, New Mexico, and Utah were also important sources of solid fuels.[4]

Colorado was the West's leading producer of coal for several decades, and the evolution of the mining industry in the Centennial State was in many ways typical of the activity that occurred throughout the region. Early settlers excavated numerous outcrops, or exposed seams. Small mines, opened in the 1860s, satisfied the demand for domestic fuel, particularly in areas where timber was scarce or nonexistent.[5] The quality of the product varied from black lignite in the northern fields to coking-grade coal in the southern fields of the territory. Shallow seams made the extraction easy, but the price was high—almost exorbitant—for consumers in distant communities. Freight costs, complicated by the seasonal nature of demand, discouraged large-scale use. These impediments of growth were largely overcome with the appearance of the railroad.

Coal was a magnet that attracted railroads. It provided fuel for locomotives as well as a source of traffic with which to generate revenues. It was not surprising, therefore, that rail carriers were instrumental in developing the commercial potential of coal throughout the West. The Northern Pacific, Great Northern, and Milwaukee Road opened mines in Montana;[6] the Union Pacific performed similar roles in Wyoming and Utah;[7] the Denver and Rio Grande Western inaugurated large-scale mining in Utah's eastern counties;[8] and the Atchison, Topeka and Santa Fe established mining enterprises at Raton and Madrid (south of Santa Fe), and encouraged others near Gallup, New Mexico.[9]

All major deposits along the eastern slope of the Rocky Mountains were targets of railroad construction schemes. The principal mining towns in the Northeast—Erie, Lafayette, Louisville, and Marshall—were linked by rail with Denver, the region's burgeoning urban-industrial center. Farther south, carriers penetrated the lignite beds near Colorado Springs and

the bituminous fields in the vicinity of Canon City. The
Atchison, Topeka and Santa Fe; the Chicago Burlington and
Quincy; the Chicago, Rock Island and Pacific; and the Denver
Texas and Fort Worth lines tapped, usually by means of
subsidiaries or affiliates, the rich steam and coking coal
resources of Huerfano and Las Animas counties. The southern
field's superior fuels were much in demand, creating a bright
prospect for large-volume shipments. That inducement, in part,
caused railroads to take the initiative in developing mines and
the communities to support activities that included extracting,
processing, and shipping solid fuel.[10]

Ancillaries of the Denver and Rio Grande Railway were the
first to develop commercially the coal resources south of the
Arkansas River. In 1872 the Central Colorado Improvement
Company opened a mine at Coal Creek in what came to be
known as the Canon District in Fremont County. In 1877 the
Southern Colorado Coal and Town Company inaugurated the
extraction of coal at Walsenburg and at Engleville, southeast of
Trinidad. Near the latter community, at the terminus of the
D&RG's southern branch, the enterprise erected beehive ovens
in which to make coke for the region's emerging smelting
industry.[11]

The driving force behind the Denver and Rio Grande was
General William Jackson Palmer. A veteran of the Union
Army, he had supervised construction of the final segment of
the Kansas Pacific to Denver in 1870. When that company
refused to extend the projected transcontinental line beyond
Colorado's territorial capital, Palmer decided to undertake a
separate construction scheme for a railroad between Denver
and the Mexican border. Supported by eastern and European
investors, Palmer built a narrow-gauge line to Colorado
Springs and Pueblo in 1872. Branches were extended from the
latter point up the Arkansas Valley to coal banks near Canon
City, and southward to the Cucharas and Purgatoire valleys
where coal abounded. The push to El Paso ended near Trinidad
when the rival Atchison, Topeka and Santa Fe Railroad gained
exclusive access to the pass over Raton Mountain, straddling
the Colorado and New Mexico border.[12]

Dr. William Abraham Bell, an English physician and cofounder of the Denver and Rio Grande, insisted that land speculation, townbuilding, and coal mining were, in the absence of public funds, means by which the line could be extended into areas of the West where it might not otherwise venture. Under Bell's guidance, the narrow gauge opened valuable coking coal deposits, erected ovens, and created towns. Alamosa, La Veta, Crested Butte, Durango, and El Moro were products of the railroad's community-building schemes; of that number, two were devoted to coal mining and another to the manufacture of coke.[13]

The Denver and Rio Grande built a successful regional transportation system partly because its promoters took advantage of abundant coal resources in the areas traversed by the narrow-gauge railway. Ancillary enterprises secured large tracts of fuel deposits in southern Colorado on both sides of the Continental Divide. Affiliated corporations took advantage of laws designed to encourage settlement and the growth of agriculture to obtain at modest costs thousands of acres of coal land. Fraud of this kind was widely practiced in the West. The Pre-emption, Homestead, and Timber and Culture Acts were used to secure fuel resources, and federal courts, by upholding the doctrine of innocent purchase, for several years made it difficult if not impossible to prevent the plundering of the public domain by speculators and promoters, including coal operators and railroads.[14]

The availability of coal, transportation services, and other resources, including iron ore and water, influenced the officers of the Denver and Rio Grande to build an integrated iron and steel plant in Colorado. The narrow gauge's ancillaries were combined in 1880 to form the Colorado Coal and Iron Company for the purpose of erecting and operating a metallurgical plant adjacent to the carrier's right of way south of Pueblo. A blast furnace, pneumatic converters, rolling mills, and related facilities were erected at the new town of Bessemer. The products were foundry and merchant iron, plus a variety of cast and rolled iron and steel goods, including rails for the region's mines and railroads.[15]

The Colorado Coal and Iron Company experienced strong competition in the metallurgical and fuel trades. Technologically more advanced eastern mills enjoyed price advantages in the western market partly because of sizeable reductions in interregional freight rates. For that reason, the Pueblo plant was operated only sporadically, forcing the enterprise to rely on coal mining for profits. However, its leadership role as a fuel producer was challenged by a newcomer, the Colorado Fuel Company, whose chief executive officer, John Cleveland Osgood, enjoyed a close working relationship with the Chicago, Burlington and Quincy Railroad. Mismanagement undermined the older firm's financial standing, enabling Osgood to negotiate a consolidation from which emerged the Colorado Fuel and Iron Company in 1892.[16]

The new corporation dominated the region's fuel trade partly because it became the principal supplier of coal to railroads. The Santa Fe, for example, leased its mines to the Colorado Fuel and Iron Company in 1896 in return for long-term contracts that assured ample supplies of fuel at reasonable cost. This allowed the carrier to devote its resources to transportation services. The Chicago, Rock Island and Pacific Railway and the Colorado Midland had by that date relinquished their mining interests to Osgood's corporation. Other trunk lines and smaller roads preferred to avoid expensive and potentially troublesome peripheral activities.[17]

Mining operations required large investments. Much capital had to be devoted to underground workings, hoisting machinery, and tipples for sorting and loading coal in railroad cars. At mines far removed from population centers, additional funds had to be allocated for the construction of structures to support employees. Company towns comprised dwellings for miners and their families, boarding houses for single men, schools, retail stores, medical offices, and recreational halls.[18]

Operators owned company towns and sometimes ran them as feudal fiefs. Local superintendents were often benevolent despots at best, and at worst they were petty tyrants. They dictated who worked in the mines and, within the framework of company policies, the conditions of employment. They influenced, or attempted to shape, the political views and voting habits of workers, and they steadfastly resisted efforts to unionize the local work force.[19]

The definitive study of company-owned communities in the western United States, James B. Allen's *The Company Town in the American West*, identified nearly two hundred in eleven states and territories. They were devoted to a variety of pursuits: agriculture, lumbering, manufacturing, milling of metallic ores, mining, petroleum production and refining, and smelting. Allen, lacking information that has come to light recently about some regions, misjudged the number of company towns. In Colorado, for example, he found only thirty-seven when in fact there were in excess of one hundred. The overwhelming proportion of these were coal-mining camps.[20]

The company town differed from traditional working-class communities in that they were created by a single enterprise for the purpose of carrying on specific industrial activities. Within the limits of the community and sometimes beyond, all land was owned by the one employer. All structures were erected by the company and reserved for its exclusive use. Schools were on occasion built by the enterprise and turned over to the board of education representing the local district. Churches were erected by particular faiths on company land and, more often than not, with large contributions from the landowner. Saloons served as social clubs. Some companies assigned the dispensing of alcoholic beverages to club houses in an effort to curb excessive drinking. Clubs also provided the only opportunities for community cultural and recreational programs.[21]

Residents of company towns were, by the close of the nineteenth century, overwhelmingly new immigrants. Initially, Colorado coal mines had been worked by native Americans, English, Welsh, and Scottish miners. The British character of the camps was diluted with the appearance of large numbers of Italians, the vanguard of immigrants arriving at a time of labor disturbances in the 1880s. The newcomers were the first of several ethnic groups that had their origins in southern and eastern Europe. Slavs, who were widely known as Austrians because they came mostly from the Austro-Hungarian Empire, were followed by other groups. Orientals had little impact on coal mining in the West, although some Chinese were employed in Wyoming and elsewhere until forced to flee because of disruptive riots in the mid-1880s.[22]

The ethnic composition of some communities was very diverse. The Colorado Fuel and Iron Company identified thirty "nationalities" among its mill and mine employees. The largest elements were native Americans, Austrians, and Italians, comprising, in all, more than half of the work force. Other sizable groups (in descending order of numbers) were Mexicans, Irish, English, Negroes, Hungarians, Welsh, Scots, Germans, Poles, Greeks, French, and Swiss. There were also small numbers of Belgians, Finns, Bohemians, Hollanders, Russians, Norwegians, Spaniards, Danes, and North American Indians.[23]

Cheap labor in the form of southern and eastern Europeans enabled the mining companies to open additional coal resources in Colorado and to expand production in spite of intensifying competition from the petroleum industry. By the opening decade of the twentieth century, immigrants were employed under conditions that at times invited trouble. Inexperienced men working in unfamiliar underground entries and roadways, ineffective communication due to the lack of a common language, and attempts to maximize output while minimizing costs led inevitably to rising levels of accidents and mounting tensions between labor and management.[24]

Numerous accidents, some of tragic proportions, stimulated interest in public regulation of coal-mining activities. A coalition of reform-minded organizations in Illinois, Ohio, and Pennsylvania, the nation's leading coal-producing states, spearheaded agitation for mine safety. The result was the formation of the United States Bureau of Mines in the Department of Interior, and widespread efforts to secure uniform state laws requiring regular inspection of mines. William Graebner, author of *Coal Mining Safety in the Progressive Period: The Political Economy of Reform*, points out that the bureau failed in the short run to diminish the hazards of coal mining. It was only a symbol of reform, lacking powers to impose substantive reforms. The miners union, operators, and bureaucrats were concerned more with their own well-being than in the achievement of meaningful safeguards against industrial accidents in underground mines.[25]

Industrial safety, as well as better working conditions and higher wages, were goals miners expected to gain not through governmental intervention but by collective bargaining. Attempts to unionize the coal-mining industry after the turn of the century were accompanied by frequent strikes, none of which were successful in the West. Tension between labor and management heightened at a time when operators experienced a downward trend in the demand for coal because of competition from so-called "clean fuels." Convinced that concessions of any kind would further undermine the competitiveness of the solid fuel in the market place, mine owners and managers refused to negotiate with disgruntled employees. In the absence of any willingness by the two groups to compromise, violence was inevitable. It was in this context that the walkout of 1913-14 culminated in the event known to organized labor as the Ludlow Massacre.[26]

Adverse reaction undermined the United Mine Workers' standing and opened the way in Colorado and elsewhere for experiments with welfare capitalism. John D. Rockefeller, Jr., shocked by the magnitude of the violence and an apparent absence of any harmony between labor and management, offered employees of the Colorado Fuel and Iron Company an industrial representation plan. A company union established channels of communications between workers and officials of the corporation, which, in an effort to secure long-term allegiance, instituted a variety of programs. These ranged from health care to educational and recreational programs.[27]

Welfare capitalism was widely adopted in the West after World War I as an instrument for combatting the growth of independent labor unions. However, industrial representation did not lessen the frequency and intensity of conflict between miners and operators. Recurring strikes reflected unrest, much of which arose from changes taking place within the fuel trade. Bituminous coal mining was a "sick industry." Excessive capacity, a problem for many years, was made even more critical when traditional consumers of coal turned to alternative fuels. Declining demand from railroads, industries, and householders meant fewer employment opportunities for miners; at the same time job security, always tenuous at best, disappeared as work forces were reduced and mines closed in response to a shrinking market.[28]

Coal's share of the nation's energy market fell sharply in the first three decades of the twentieth century. Solid fuel supplied approximately 90 percent of the country's needs in 1900. This fell to 85 percent in 1910, to 78 percent in 1920, and to 63 percent in 1930. Petroleum and natural gas, in the same period, experienced sharp increases in consumption. Those fuels provided only 8 percent of the energy market in 1900 and 34 percent in 1930.[29]

Coal production in the intermountain region peaked at the close of the first decade of the century, declined over a period of five years, and climbed to record levels during and immediately following World War I. Five states—Colorado, Montana, New Mexico, Utah, and Wyoming—produced an aggregate 28.5 million tons of bituminous coal or lignite in 1910. That amount was surpassed each year from 1916 to 1920, reaching in the latter instance 36.1 million tons. At the time the Rocky Mountain states accounted for 6.33 percent of the nation's output.[30]

Coal production fell sharply again after 1920, more so in the western states than in the remainder of the country. Output in the Rocky Mountains dipped to 23.5 million tons, or 5.03 percent of the nation's total, in 1930. This downward trend continued during the depression that began in 1929. By 1934, regional output was only 15.8 million tons, or 4.4 percent of production in the United States. That year mines in the West yielded only 43.9 percent of the amount reported in 1920.[31]

The loss was attributed mainly to competition from natural gas and petroleum. The problem was further aggravated by industry's adoption of technology that enhanced the efficient consumption of fuel and by the slow rate of growth peculiar to enterprises that used large quantities of coal. Mine capacity was not adjusted to the dwindling market until beleagured operators combined under the Blue Eagle of the National Recovery Administration in 1933. Production quotas, uniform labor standards, and minimum price afforded substantial relief from the unrestrained competition that had disrupted the fuel market for more than two decades.[32]

Government-sanctioned "fair competition" convinced many operators and miners that even stricter measures were needed. Responding to pressures from producers and the United Mine Workers of America, in 1935 Congress adopted the Guffey-Snyder Act, which authorized the formation of a Coal Commission and other boards to advance the interests of miners, mine owners, and consumers. Stability was to be derived from output quotas and industry-wide price and wage scales. Workers were assured of rights to organize and to bargain collectively with employers. Before the law was fully implemented, the Supreme Court invalidated the labor pro-visions and, indirectly, the pricing arrangements.[33]

The Guffey-Vinson Act of 1937 revived in slightly modified form the fair practices provisions of the earlier law. Implemen-tation was slow until the Supreme Court, acting in 1940, ruled favorably on the price-fixing provisions of the legislation. By that time, however, the United States was strengthening its armed forces, a reaction to wars in Asia and Europe, and the heightened demand for fuel eliminated, at least temporarily, the need for curbs on competition within the coal-mining industry.[34]

Rapid expansion of coal production during World War II was followed by prolonged depression. Western output climbed to 31.1 million tons in 1944 before starting downward the following year. Production declined to fewer than 20 million tons in 1951 and dropped to fewer than 11 million tons before the close of the decade. The region's share of the national output fell from slightly more than five percent in 1944 to about 2.5 percent in 1959.[35]

In the decade and a half following World War II, what remained of the intermountain region's coal-mining industry was largely dismantled. Traditional leaders disappeared from the scene: the Utah Fuel Company, Rocky Mountain Fuel Company, Victor-American Fuel Company, and the St. Louis

Rocky Mountain and Pacific Company. The one-time giant of
the fuel trade, the Colorado Fuel and Iron Corporation,
restricted operations, in time producing only metallurgical coal
for its own consumption.[36]

Mines were gradually shut down as petroleum and natural
gas absorbed an ever-larger proportion of the fuel market. The
conversion of railroads from coal to oil was a blow from which
the Colorado Fuel and Iron Company had not recovered when
natural gas from Texas and Kansas was piped into the
Centennial State in the late 1920s. Coal's noncompetitiveness
was aggravated by widespread economic stagnation in the
1930s. The firm's fortunes revived briefly during World War II,
after which mines were closed at a rapid pace in order to adjust
output to shrinking demand. The Morley Mine, on Raton Pass
south of Trinidad, ceased operation in 1956, and four years later
the Frederick Mine closed, marking the end of the company
town in Colorado's coal fields. By 1960, the Pueblo enterprise
had produced an aggregate of 163.3 million tons of coal. Only
one property, the highly automated Allen Mine that was opened
in the valley of the Purgatoire River in 1950, continued in
production to supply the by-product coke ovens at the steel
works.[37]

A second coal-mining boom began in the West in 1960. That
year the intermountain states reported an aggregate yield of
11.2 million tons, the first increase in several years. Production
jumped to 28.8 million tons in 1970 and to 40.7 million in 1972,
exceeding that year the previous record established in 1920.
Output continued to soar, reaching 49.6 million tons in 1973
and 63.1 million in 1974. In the latter year, six Rocky Mountain
states (Arizona, Colorado, Montana, New Mexico, Utah, and
Wyoming) accounted for 10.5 percent of all the coal mined in
the United States.[38]

The revival was prompted by the rapid expansion of coal-
fired, steam-generating electric stations. New plants were built
in part to satisfy the rising demand for energy in the Rocky
Mountain region, but a high proportion of the electricity
produced in the intermountain states was transmitted to large
urban centers on the Pacific Coast. Western coal, because of its

low sulphur content, also became an important fuel for utilities in the Mississippi Valley.

The resurgence of coal mining occurred initially in the Southwest, where the Arizona Public Service Company's Four Corners plant, a mine-mouth generating facility, consumed strip-mining fuel. A 350-megawatt unit near Farmington, New Mexico, formally dedicated in the summer of 1963, was located on the Navajo Reservation, adjacent to an open-pit mine. The plant consumed 4,200 tons of coal daily. An additional 225 megawatts of capacity raised fuel consumption to 2.5 million tons a year. The electricity was transmitted to consumers in Arizona, mainly the Phoenix area.[39]

Coal was extracted from an open pit adjacent to the generating plant. The Utah Construction and Mining Company (now Utah International, Inc.) worked the mine. Overburden ranging from 10 to 120 feet in thickness was removed by a 45-cubic-yard dragline. Crushed coal delivered to the plant was sold not by the ton but in blocks of a million British thermal units.[40]

Four Corners became the model for other generating stations. Hoping to take advantage of recently developed techniques of extra-high-voltage transmission in order to obtain fuel-cost reduction from remote mine-mouth plants, several utilities organized the Western Energy Supply and Transmission Association (WEST) in September 1964. Seventeen private and public enterprises, faced with the necessity of rapidly increasing generating capacity over a period of a decade and a half, proposed to build large generating plants near available fuel resources. Two 755-megawatt units were to be erected in the Four Corners area near the Arizona Public Service Company's existing facility. The Mohave Generating Station, a 1500-megawatt unit, was to be constructed in southern Nevada on the Colorado River below Davis Dam. The Kaiparowitz Generating Station, a 3000-megawatt unit, was to be located north of Lake Powell in southern Utah. The three projects were to produce electricity for distribution in a nine-state area, including most of Arizona, Colorado, New Mexico, and Utah, plus portions of California, Idaho, Nevada,

Wyoming, and Texas.[41]

Six utilities pooled their resources to erect two large coal-fired, steam-generating plants in the Four Corners Area. Public Service Company of New Mexico, the Salt River Project (Phoenix), the Tucson Gas and Electric Company, El Paso Electric Company, and Southern California Edison Company were participants in addition to Arizona Public Service Company, the project manager. The Utah Construction and Mining Company supplied requisite fuel from the Navajo Mine, where two 50-cubic-yard draglines augmented existing equipment in order to meet the anticipated increased demand. When new generating units became operational in the early 1970s, coal production rose well above 6 million tons a year, making the Navajo Mine, for a time, the nation's largest.[42]

The Mohave generating station derived its fuel from Arizona, which did not rank among important coal-producing states until the 1970s. Southern California Edison, the project manager, contracted with Peabody Coal Company of St. Louis for a minimum of 177 million tons of coal over a period of 35 years. Peabody leased from the Navajo and Hopi tribes large deposits in the Black Mesa area. The Southern Pacific Pipeline Company, acting through a subsidiary, constructed a 273-mile-long, 18-inch line to transport slurry (coal and water) from the mine to the electrical plant in Clark County, Nevada. Shipments amounted to about 5.2 million tons of fuel a year.[43]

Peabody's Black Mesa resources also supplied the Navajo generating station erected near Glen Canyon Dam on the Colorado River. The Arizona Public Service Company, the Salt River Project, Tucson Gas and Electric Company, and the Los Angeles Department of Water and Power constructed at Page the largest electric plant in Arizona. The 2310-megawatt unit, dedicated in 1976, consumed in excess of 8 million tons of coal a year, all of which moved from mine to plant over a 78-mile-long electric railway built specifically to handle that traffic.[44]

To the north of Lake Powell, the Kaiparowitz plant, the largest in WEST's projected grid, was not built. Ample coal was available in southern Utah for underground mining to meet anticipated consumption levels of up to 14.6 million tons a year, but resistance by individuals and groups blocked industrial development in the area. Dissidents claimed that Utah's clean air and water were to be sacrificed for the benefit of energy-spendthrift cities in other states. The charge was seemingly irrefutable because most of the power to be generated was to be consumed in Arizona and southern California.[45]

Although without appreciable strippable reserves, Utah's coal-mining industry experienced a resurgence in the 1970s. Peak production had been recorded in 1944, when the yield topped 7 million tons. Output declined gradually to a low of 4.1 million tons in 1967 before rebounding to 5.5 million in 1973 and 7 million in 1975.[46] Metallurgical fuel was mined for steel production in Utah and California, but most of the output was consumed by the state's electric utilities. The Utah Power and Light Company's Huntington Canyon plant, a 430-megawatt unit opened in 1974 as part of WEST's grid, was indicative of the trend toward enlarged generating capacity.[47]

Located 30 miles southwest of Price, the power plant derived its fuel from Peabody Coal Company's Deer Creek Mine. Continuous mining machines, loaders, and shuttle cars— and a two-mile, covered belt-conveyor excavated and moved coal from two underground seams comprising an estimated 335 million ton reserve, more than enough to sustain the Huntington Canyon facility for its estimated 35-year lifetime. Initial output at the rate of 1.2 million tons a year was scheduled to rise to 5 million tons with the construction of additional generating capacity.[48]

The rapid growth of electric utilities and attendant expansion of coal mining was not unique to the Southwest. Similar development occurred throughout the Rocky Mountain region, particularly wherever strippable reserves were accessible. Large, shallow, low-sulphur coal and lignite deposits in several states attracted generating plants to the area, in addition to providing some of the fuel needs of other regions.

Montana's coal mining industry, built upon the largest reserve in the continental limits of the United States, suffered a long postwar depression before a revival began in recent years. Output, after peaking at 4.8 million tons in 1944, fell to 313,000 tons in 1960. Demand rose gradually in the next decade. By 1969, the combined yield of coal and lignite exceeded one million tons for the first time since the mid-1950s.[49] This advance was attributed mainly to stripping operations at Colstrip, Rosebud County, where Western Energy Company (a subsidiary of Montana Power Company) and Peabody Coal Company supplied the growing needs of utilities for fuel.[50]

The Pacific Northwest and the upper Middle West turned to the Treasure State for energy to sustain the quickening tempo of the economy in the 1970s. This demand was filled in part by the construction of mine-mouth, coal-fired, steam-generating plants and extra-high-voltage transmission of power to population centers in adjoining states. Montana Power Company and Puget Sound Power and Light Company initiated in 1972 a project to erect electric generating stations at Colstrip.[51] Much of the power from that complex was consumed in western Washington. At about the same time, Pacific Power and Light Company and Peter Kiewit Sons, Inc., acting through subsidiaries, combined to mine low-sulphur coal near Decker, in southeastern Montana, for distribution to utilities in the Mississippi Valley.[52] In addition, the fuel reserves underlying the Crow and Northern Cheyenne reservations attracted the attention of Peabody, Amax, Westmoreland Resources, and other enterprises, including major oil companies.[53]

Much of the recent growth in Montana's coal-mining industry has been built upon exports to utilities in the Middle West. In Chicago, Detroit, and other communities, the consumption of low-sulphur western fuel was one way of slowing the deterioration of air quality. The shuttling of unit trains to distant industrial cities boosted the output of coal and lignite from 3.4 million tons in 1970 to 13.8 million in 1974.[54] Output continued upward in response to the oil embargo of 1973-74, the worsening of the energy crisis, and the deliberate shift of power stations and other large consumers of fuel from local to western coal.

The impact of the energy crisis was even more visible in Wyoming, the Rocky Mountain region's leader in the production of coal. The large-scale consumption of the state's coal for the generation of electricity for distribution to other states began in 1958, when Pacific Power and Light Company placed in operation its Dave Johnson plant near Casper. Thereafter, the resurgence of coal mining paralleled for some years increases in power-producing capacities of the region's utilities.[55]

Coal production had fallen to a postwar low of 1.6 million tons in 1958 before rebounding, reaching 7.2 million tons in 1970 and 20.7 million in 1974. Forecasts call for even more dramatic growth in the future. The Wyoming Geological Survey predicts that the yield will jump to 125 million tons by 1987, nearly all of which will be consumed by utilities in the Far West and Middle West.[56] In the Powder River Basin alone, output will climb to at least 86 million tons by the mid-1980s.[57] There Atlantic-Richfield, Amax, Carter, Kerr-McGee, and Sunoco have large-scale operations. Amax Coal Company anticipates that its two open pits will turn out 35 million tons a year by 1985. That firm has long-term contracts to supply power plants in Arkansas, Colorado, Indiana, Iowa, Kansas, Missouri, and Texas.[58]

In Colorado, as in its neighbor to the north, a coal boom was touched off by the rapid expansion of electric-generating capacity. Most of the advance in output came from strippable reserves. In one northwestern county, three companies operating surface mines produced in 1976 an aggregate of 5.5 million tons of coal, or 58 percent of the state's total yield.[59] The Pittsburgh and Midway Coal Mining Company (Gulf Oil), Energy Fuels Corporation, and Seneca Coals, Ltd. (Peabody) were the chief suppliers of Colorado Ute Electric Association and Public Service Company of Colorado, the largest utilities in the Centennial State. Rising demand within and outside Colorado, particularly from power plants, may push production in Routt, Rio Blanco, and Moffat counties to 25 million tons by 1980 and to 33 million by 1990.[60]

The current coal-mining boom in the West differs in many respects from the earlier period of rapid growth. In the late nineteenth century, mining was restricted to underground workings, where labor-intensive methods of extraction prevailed. The principal consumers of fuel were railroads, industries, and households, in that order. Since 1960, production has centered more and more in surface mines. Extraction above or below ground is capital intensive, with machines and heavy equipment supplanting most human labor. Electric utilities are the major consumers of fuel, followed—at least in Colorado, New Mexico, and Utah—by the steelmakers. Metallurgical coal, shipped formerly only to the integrated iron and steel plant at Pueblo, Colorado, is now consumed in large quantities by the United States Steel Corporation's Geneva Works in Utah and by the Kaiser Steel Corporation's Fontana Works in California.[61]

The current emphasis on surface mining in the West takes advantage of the region's substantial reserves of fuel located at shallow depths. Somewhat more than half of the nation's strippable deposits are in the intermountain states, with the heaviest concentrations in Montana and Wyoming, in that order.[62] Open-pit mines produce a large volume of coal at relatively low cost because of almost complete recovery of the resource and high labor productivity. In Colorado, for example, 330 men were employed in surface operations in 1976, compared to 1,382 in underground workings. The former produced 6.1 million tons while the latter recorded 3.3 million. Output per unit of labor favored surface over subsurface mining by a margin of 18,514 to 2,433 tons.[63]

America's largest mines are open pits, and the most productive ones are in the Rocky Mountain region. The Navajo Mine, in northwestern New Mexico, ranked first in output in 1970.[64] The Deckers Coal Company's number one mine moved to the top by 1976. That year, eight of the leading ten producers in the United States were in four intermountain states. Deckers and Western Energy Company's Colstrip led all rivals, followed, in order, by Amax Coal Company's Belle Ayr Mine in Wyoming, Utah International's Navajo Mine, and Peabody Coal Company's Black Mesa Mine. The latter's Kayenta Mine (Black Mesa No. 2) ranked seventh, and Westmoreland Resources' Absaloka Mine, located on the Crow Reservation in Montana, was ninth. The seven western mines reported an aggregate output of 53 million tons, accounting for 8 percent of the nation's coal production.[65]

Today, as at the time of the earlier boom, most of the coal reserves in the Rocky Mountain region are on federal land or Indian reservations. A century ago, when the industry was unregulated and competitive, fuel deposits were readily available in seemingly unlimited quantities, and the easiest way to acquire them was by purchase or other means from the public domain. Mining operations are now strictly regulated for the safety of workers, and competition has been for all practical purposes eliminated by reason of the small number of large producers and demand that runs ahead of supply. Since 1920, public land containing coal, as well as other minerals, can be leased but not purchased or otherwise acquired outright from the government.[66] In recent years, federal laws designed to protect the quality of the environment at the mine site as well as the place where coal is consumed has made the leasing of deposits, the operation of mines, and the consumption of fossil fuel a matter of public control. These statutes have been seized upon by critics of industrial development who, for whatever reasons, hope to block, or at least delay, the expansion of energy-related industries in the West. Most statutes were intended only to protect the environment and preserve the culture, lifestyle, and health of area residents.[67]

The vulnerability of the mining industry has been made abundantly clear by recent actions of the Environmental Protection Agency. The construction of coal-fired, electric-generating plants at Colstrip, and elsewhere, has been blocked on the grounds that they pose a threat to air quality standards.[68] This may prevent the erection of additional mine-mouth generating stations to supply power for communities outside the Rocky Mountain region. At the same time, the shipment of fuel in large volume from the intermountain states to the Middle West and South is jeopardized by a recent amendment to the Clean Air Act, which, if fully implemented, will require the installation of scrubbers on all coal-fired power plants. Utilities, without regard for the nature of the coal they burn, will have to remove 85 percent of sulphur dioxide fumes from stack gases

before they enter the atmosphere. Until now, low-sulphur
western coal has been an acceptable substitute for the cleaning
equipment. If that expensive technology has to be adopted,
power companies may prefer to burn eastern or middle western
coals which, although high in sulphur, have greater heat
values.[69]

Coal is America's premier energy resource, and the Rocky
Mountain region contains a sizable proportion of the nation's
known and estimated reserves. A slowing in the construction of
utilities or in the growth of coal shipments to the Middle West
and South will not end the mining boom that has occurred in
many parts of the intermountain states in the past two decades.
The high price of imported petroleum and the dwindling
supplies of natural gas may in fact force industries to undertake
massive conversions to the solid fuel, setting off a new and more
active round of mine development in response to the rising
demand for low-sulphur coal.

Notes

1. United States Geological Survey, Mineral Resources of the
United States, 1900 (Washington: Government Printing Office, 1901),
pp. 368-71, 373, 406-11, 441-43, 454-57.

2. Ibid., 1910, 2 vols. (Washington: Government Printing Office
1911), 2:26.

3. Paul Averitt, Coal Resources of the United States, January 1,
1974. USGS Bulletin, no. 142 (Washington: Government Printing
Office, 1975), p. 5.

4. United States Geological Survey, Mineral Resources of the
United States 1910, 2:33. New Mexico, Montana, and Utah ranked
16th, 18th, and 20th, respectively, among coal producing states in
1910.

5. LeRoy R. Hafen, ed., *Colorado and Its People: A Narrative and Topical History of the Centennial State*, 4 vols. (New York: Lewis Historical Publ. Co., 1948), 1:449; Maynard A. Peck, "Some Economic Aspects of the Coal Industry in Boulder County, Colorado" (Ph.D. diss., University of Colorado, Boulder, 1947), pp. 5-6, 10.

6. Merrill G. Burlingame and K. Ross Toole, *A History of Montana*, 2 vols. (New York: Lewis Historical Publ., 1957), 1:361-65, 2:155, 171; Michael Malone and Richard B. Roeder, *Montana: A History of Two Centuries* (Seattle: University of Washington Press, 1976), p. 258.

7. Thomas G. Alexander, "From Dearth to Deluge: Utah's Coal Industry," *Utah Historical Quarterly* 31 (Summer 1963): 237; George B. Pryde, "The Union Pacific Coal Company, 1868 to August 1952," *Annals of Wyoming* 25 (July 1952): 191-92.

8. Alexander, "From Dearth to Deluge," p. 237.

9. Ralph Emerson Twitchell, ed., *Leading Facts of New Mexico's History*, 5 vols. (Cedar Rapids, Iowa: The Torch Press, 1911-17), 3:64, 376-77.

10. The construction of railroads is discussed at length in Herbert O. Bayer, "History of Colorado Railroads," in Hafen, ed., *Colorado and Its People*, 2:635-90.

11. H. Lee Scamehorn, *Pioneer Steelmaker in the West*. (Boulder, Colo.: Pruett, 1976). Denver and Rio Grande Railway, chartered in Colorado, and the Denver and Rio Grande Western Railway, chartered in Utah, had largely the same stockholders and were controlled by General William Jackson Palmer and his associates.

12. Robert G. Athearn, *Rebel of the Rockies: The Denver and Rio Grande Western Railroad* (New Haven: Yale University Press, 1962), chaps. 1-4. See also Scamehorn, *Pioneer Steelmaker in the West*, chaps. 2-3.

13. Scamehorn, *Pioneer Steelmaker in the West*, pp. 29-30, 50, 83. See also John S. Fisher, *A Builder of the West: The Life of General William Jackson Palmer* (Caldwell, Idaho: The Caxton Printers, 1939), pp. 249, 261-63.

14. Scamehorn, *Pioneer Steelmaker in the West*, pp. 51-52, 69, 83-84. See also Harold H. Dunham, *Government Handout: A Study of the Administration of Public Lands, 1875-1891* (New York: De Capo Press, 1970), pp. 204-11.

15. Scamehorn, *Pioneer Steelmaker in the West*, pp. 45-49.

16. Ibid., pp. 90-92.

17. Ibid., pp. 85-86, 88-90, 121-22.

18. Ibid., pp. 149-50.

19. George S. McGovern and Leonard F. Guttridge, *The Great Coalfield War* (Boston: Houghton Mifflin Co., 1972), pp. 8-9, 23-24, 28-29; Barron B. Beshoar, *Out of the Depths: The Story of John Lawson, a Labor Leader* (Denver: The World Press, 1942), pp. 1-3.

20. James B. Allen, *The Company Towns in the American West* (Norman: University of Oklahoma Press, 1966), pp. 156-60. The author's estimate of company towns in Colorado is based upon a study of those communities in the southern and northwestern fields.

21. Allen, *Company Towns in the American West*, pp. 57-64; Scamehorn, *Pioneer Steelmaker in the West*, chap. 11.

22. Scamehorn, *Pioneer Steelmaker in the West*, p. 150. The reaction to Chinese coal miners in Wyoming is discussed in T. A. Larson, *Wyoming: A Bicentennial History* (New York: W. W. Norton & Co., Nashville: American Association for State and Local History, 1977), pp. 146-47.

23. See articles in *Camp and Plant*, "The Austrian Slavs of Pueblo," 2 (27 December 1903): 622-23, and A. E. Matthews, "Methods of Keeping Payrolls and Paying Employees," 3 (18 April 1903): 345.

24. William Graebner, *Coal Mining Safety in the Progressive Period: The Political Economy of Reform* (Lexington: University of Kentucky Press, 1976), pp. 2, 117-23.

25. Ibid., pp. 4-10.

26. Two studies of the coal miners' strike of 1913-14, written from the perspective of organized labor, are Beshoar, *Out of the Depths*, and McGovern and Guttridge, *The Great Coalfield War*. See also Irving Bernstein, *The Lean Years: A History of the American Worker 1920-33* (Boston: Houghton Mifflin Co., 1960), pp. 157-58.

27. Scamehorn, *Pioneer Steelmaker in the West*, pp. 171-73; Bernstein, *The Lean Years*, pp. 159-65.

28. The impact of declining demand for coal on the Colorado Fuel and Iron Company is discussed in Scamehorn, *Pioneer Steelmaker in the West*, pp. 170-73. A diagnosis of bituminous coal mining as a sick industry after World War I is in Ralph Hills Baker, *The National Bituminous Coal Commission: Administration of the Bituminous Coal Act, 1937-41* (Baltimore: The Johns Hopkins Press, 1941), pp. 13-37.

29. U. S. Bureau of Mines, *Mineral Resources of the United States, 1930*, 2 vols. (Washington: Government Printing Office, 1932), 2:622-23.

30. Ibid., *1925*, 2 vols., 2: 528-33.

31. Ibid., *1935*, p. 630.

32. Baker, *The National Bituminous Coal Commission*, pp. 43-48; Ellis W. Hawley, *The New Deal and the Problem of Monopoly: A Study in Economic Ambivalence* (Princeton, N. J.: Princeton University Press, 1966), p. 206.

33. Baker, *The National Bituminous Coal Commission*, pp. 40-62, 268-75; Hawley, *The New Deal and the Problem of Monopoly*, pp. 207-9.

34. Baker, *The National Bituminous Coal Commission*, pp. 63-80, 138-88, 275-76; Hawley, *The New Deal and the Problem of Monopoly*, pp. 209-10.

35. U. S. Bureau of Mines, *Minerals Yearbook, 1945* (Washington: Government Printing Office, 1947), p. 855; *Minerals Yearbook, 1959*, 2:55.

36. Claude P. Heiner, "The First 100 Years—A Story of Utah Coal," typescript in Utah Fuel Company Collection, Archives and Manuscripts Department, Harold B. Lee Library, Brigham Young University, Provo, Utah. The Utah Fuel Company sold its property in 1950 to the Kaiser Steel Corporation. Colorado Coal Mine Inspection Department, *Annual Report, 1944-46* (Denver, 1947), pp. 43-44, 278; *Annual Report, 1947-49*, pp. 49-50. The Rocky Mountain Fuel Company closed its last two mines in 1945 and 1946. *Engineering and Mining Journal* 104 (7 July 1917): 38; Colorado Coal Mine Inspection Department, *Annual Report, 1950-53*, pp. 44-45, 54-55; *Annual Report, 1954*, pp. 56-57. The Victor-American Fuel Company sold its properties at Gallup, New Mexico, in 1917, and closed the last of its Colorado mines in 1953 and 1954. Jerry Steven Segotta, "A History of the St. Louis, Rocky Mountain and Pacific Company" (thesis, New Mexico Highlands University, Las Vegas, 1970), p. 91. The St Louis, Rocky Mountain and Pacific Company sold its mines in Colfax County, New Mexico, to the Kaiser Steel Corporation in 1955.

37. Colorado Coal Mine Inspection Department, *Annual Report, 1956*, p. 1; *Annual Report, 1961*, p. 2. The CF&I Corporation's aggregate production for the years from 1872 to 1960 is computed from company data and the Colorado Coal Mine Inspector's annual or biennial reports since 1884.

38. Statistics are taken from U. S. Bureau of Mines, *Mineral Resources of the United States, 1960-74.*

39. "APS's Four Corners Plant," *Electrical West* 130 (August 1963): 22; *Minerals Yearbook, 1963*, 3:744; *Minerals Yearbook, 1964*, 3:686.

40. "Construction Plans for WEST's Four Corners Plant," *Electrical West* 133 (February 1966): 59, 61-62; *Minerals Yearbook, 1967*, 3:556.

41. "Construction Plans for WEST's Four Corner's Plant," pp. 51, 61-62. See additional articles in *Electrical West*: "Coal's Western Power Role," 132 (August 1965): 22; "Plans Advance for WEST's Projects," 133 (June 1966): 63; "Generation, Fuel Energy Flow Are Big Challenges for WEST Groups," 133 (September 1966): 50-51, 55; "Progress Reported on WEST Projects," 133 (December 1966): 23; "WEST Construction Projects Moving Ahead," 134 (September 1967): 52-53.

42. Paul Averitt, *Stripping-Coal Resources of the United States, January 1, 1970.* USGS *Bulletin* no. 1322 (Washington: Government Printing Office, 1970), p. 16; Robert C. Bellas, "New Mexico," *Coal Age* 78 (Mid-April 1978): 126, and "New Mexico: State Still Boasts Nation's Largest Surface Mine," *Coal Age* 79 (May 1974): 89-90; D. W. Reeves "WEST Concept Captures Public's Imagination," *Electrical West* 133 (September 1966): 49, 55; William B. Loper, "Generation, Fuel, Energy Flow Are Big Challenges to WEST Groups," *Electrical West* 133 (September 1966): 50-51, 55.

43. Averitt, *Stripping-Coal Resources of the United States*, p. 10; Bellas, "Arizona," pp. 78-79, and "Arizona: Coal Moves," p. 77; "Large Coal Reserves Secured for New "WEST" Generating Plant," *Electrical West* 132 (November 1965): 35; "Mohave Project Rising in Nevada Desert," *Electrical West* 136 (March 1969): 34.

44. Averitt, *Stripping-Coal Resources*, pp. 10-11; Bellas, "Arizona: Coal Moves," p. 78; "The Black Mesa Plan: Energy Today, Better Land Tomorrow," *Coal Age* 76 (March 1971): 78-82; "Lease Agreement Signed for Arizona's Largest Powerplant," *Electrical West* 136 (November 1969): 15-16.

45. *Denver Post*, 5 October 1975, p. 30; 4 April 1976, p. 4; 11 April 1976, p. 29, 41; 25 May 1976, p. 4.

46. *Minerals Yearbook, 1950*, p. 275; *Minerals Yearbook, 1968*, 3:740; *Minerals Yearbook, 1973*, 2:711-12.

47. John W. Shepardson, "Utah," *Coal Age* 78 (Mid-April 1973): 169; Harold Schindler, "Utah: Producers Brace for 300% Jump in Output," *Coal Age* 79 (May 1974): 95; "UP&L Building Program Is Largest in History," *Electrical West* 137 (July 1970): 16.

48. *Coal Age* 75 (July 1970): 46; Schindler, "Utah: Producers Brace for 300% Jump in Output," p. 95.

49. *Minerals Yearbook, 1950*, p. 275; *1961*, p. 98; *1969*, 3:463-64.

50. Averitt, *Stripping-Coal Resources*, p. 16; Joe R. Rawlins, "Montana," *Coal Age* 78 (Mid-April, 1973): 18-19; *Minerals Yearbook, 1969*, 3:463; *1972*, 2:433.

51. Rawlins, "Montana," p. 118.

52. Ibid., pp. 118-19. See also *Coal Age* 75 (July 1970): 46; 77 (October 1972): 47; and 82 (December 1977): 51.

53. Joe R. Rawlins, "Montana: Legislators Give the State Control Over Surface Mine Sitings," *Coal Age* 79 (May 1974): 87; Dan Jackson, "Montana-Based Westmoreland Resources Mines Crow Indian-Owned Coal at Absaloka Mine," *Coal Age* 80 (December 1975): 66-73.

54. *Minerals Yearbook, 1970*, 2:436-37; *1974*, 2:429-30.

55. "Rocky Mountains Largest Steam Unit Dedicated," *Electrical West*, 131 (November 1964): 34; "Coal Has Growing Role in West," *Electrical West* 132 (April 1965): 44.

56. *Denver Post*, 16 July 1978, p. 37.

57. Garry B. Glass, "Wyoming: Production Seen Doubling by 1976," *Coal Age* 79 (May 1974): 102.

58. "Amax Sees Record Production: Eagle Butte Opening," *Coal Age* 82 (October 1977): 23.

59. Colorado Department of Natural Resources, Division of Mines, *A Summary of Mineral Industry Activities in Colorado, 1976*, pt. 1: *Coal* (Denver, 1977), p. 25.

60. U. S. Department of the Interior, Bureau of Land Management, *Final Environmental Statement Northwest Colorado: Regional Analysis*, 4 vols. (Washington: Government Printing Office, 1976), p. 1-2.

61. Shepardson, "Utah," p. 163; Bellas, "New Mexico: State Still Boasts Nation's Largest Surface Coal Mine," p. 91; Robeck, "Colorado: Energy Shortages Prompt New Look at Potential Coal Markets," p. 81.

62. Averitt, *Stripping-Coal Resources*, p. 23.

63. Colorado Department of Natural Resources, Division of Mines, *A Summary of Mineral Industry Activities in Colorado, 1976*, pt. 1: *Coal*, p. 20.

64. "The 50 Largest Bituminous Mines of 1970," *Coal Age* 76 (April 1971): 117.

65. Ibid., 82 (May 1977): 43.

66. Roy M. Robbins, *Our Landed Heritage: The Public Domain, 1776-1963* (Gloucester, Mass.: Peter Smith, 1960), pp. 394-95.

67. Critical accounts of the growth of coal mining in the West are Malcolm F. Baldwin, *The Southwest Energy Complex: A Policy Evaluation* (Washington, D. C.: The Conservation Foundation, 1973); Suzanne Gordon, *Black Mesa: Angel of Death* (New York: The John Day Company, 1973); and K. Ross Toole, *The Rape of the Great Plains: Northwest America, Cattle and Coal* (Boston: Little, Brown and Co., 1976).

68. *Denver Post*, 15 June 1978, p. 36; 20 August 1978, p. 16.

69. Ibid., 17 September 1978, pp. 1, 16.

The Transformation of Utah's Agriculture, 1847-1900

Davis Bitton and Linda Wilcox

Since 1920 was the first year after 1870 that the census report showed Utah's agricultural employment to exceed the national average, an understanding of the transformation of agriculture in the late nineteenth century is of great importance. In the following essay, Davis Bitton, Professor of History at the University of Utah, and Linda Wilcox, a private researcher from Salt Lake City, argue that the introduction of new plant strains and agricultural machinery facilitated this transformation.

Organizations and individuals in the territory, fostered by private associations, territorial government, and the LDS Church, helped to bring these changes about. Church and community leaders preached, wrote, and promoted, and organizations like the Deseret Agricultural and Manufacturing Society helped to facilitate the dissemination of information about plants and machines. Not until the 1870s did harvesting machines make much of a dent in the Utah market. Interestingly enough, it was after 1870 that the percentage of those employed in Utah agriculture began to slip below the national average.

The absolute number of those engaged in various agricultural activities increased, however, and most important, the new machinery allowed fewer farmers to produce more by occupying and cultivating more land. Thus, from 1850 to 1900 the number of farms increased twenty times while the amount of land in

*farms increased by eighty-five times, allowing each farmer to be
much more productive.*

During the second half of the nineteenth century all of
America was undergoing profound change. This was true of
agriculture as well as manufacturing and commerce. The
expanded population meant greater need for food; the
westward thrust of expansion meant increased lands that could
be cultivated; the mechanization of agriculture, most often
associated with Cyrus McCormick's reaper, meant that more
acres could be cultivated more efficiently; and the railroad
revolution greatly increased the possibility of specialized
regional production and marketing crops and livestock outside
the immediate locality in which the farmer lived.

During the same half century Utah underwent substantially
the same transformation. It was a microcosm of the national
macrocosm, repeating the experience in Iowa, Oregon,
Colorado, and California. Still, there were some differences.
For one thing, the starting point was lower than almost
anywhere else. Irrigation became an indispensable foundation
to agriculture in Utah, which differentiated the experience from
that in most farming areas of the country. It took place in what
can be generally described as a religious community, the great
majority of Utah's farmers being Mormons. Perhaps because
the struggle between church and national government so
naturally occupied the center of the stage, the changes in Utah's
agriculture have never received the attention they deserve.[1]

Just how phenomenal Utah's agricultural growth was is
evident when we look at the increases in production during the
second half of the nineteenth century. Compared to 1850,
production of basic farm crops in 1900 had multiplied from 25
to nearly 180 times. The 926 farms in Utah in 1850 had
multiplied to over 19,000, while the acres of farm land had
increased from not quite 47,000 to more than 4 million. The
population of Utah was growing rapidly as a result of both
natural increase and immigration. But although the population

multiplied by about 30 times from 1850 to 1900, the agricultural productivity far outstripped the rate of population growth.

The process we will review here falls naturally into three periods. First was the real pioneering generation lasting from 1847 to 1869. The population was still thin; the areas under cultivation were still the most obvious locations—the Wasatch Front, Weber and Cache Valleys, and a few other settlements—with the Dixie Mission having opened up a kind of outpost. Second was the period of just over twenty years extending from 1869 to 1890. This was a period of continued population growth, improved transportation within Utah, much greater contact with the "outside world," and the continued establishment of settlements in places like Randolph, Cannonville, Grouse Creek, and Price (and beyond Utah in Idaho and Arizona). Then, at the close of the century, during the 1890s, occurred the most phenomenal burst of agricultural expansion ever experienced in the state. Coinciding with continued population growth, agriculture expanded its production. It was a decade of unprecedented diversification, mechanization, and market development.

The settlers of early Utah had several feats to perform in order to accomplish their agricultural miracle. They had to get people to settle an area that on the surface was not particularly inviting, not only in 1847 but throughout the century. They had to get water onto the soil in order for crops to survive the arid environment. They had to get word to each other of the best kinds of crops to grow and when to plant and harvest. They had, as soon as possible, to bring in machinery that would enable them to do more with less manpower, for cultivating farms without machinery meant back-breaking drudgery that could quickly break spirits. In all of this they had to maintain some kind of psychological momentum that would counteract the constantly threatening discouragement and tedium. They somehow had to combat the hordes of insects that came in during some years to wipe out crops and create famine. To indulge in a little alliteration, the Utah farmers had to overcome desolation, dryness, dearth of information, drudgery, discouragement—and those damned grasshoppers.

In attracting converts to the West, the Mormons found it important to make the fertility of the area sound as attractive as possible. In letters from Utah to Europe, in church periodicals, and in specific promotional documents, the fertility and productivity of Utah were eulogized. This happened not only with respect to the area in general, but also for each little settlement as it was trying to become established. Daniel Boorstin noted that in 1786 Pittsburgh was a mere village of three hundred, but to the eyes of the booster it was "a great metropolis in embryo."[2] The same was true of Salt Lake City in 1847 and 1848, of Parowan in 1850, and of Grouse Creek in 1878. Consider the impact of the following on a believing Latter-day Saint living in poverty in Scandinavia or Manchester:

> The grain crops in the valley have been good this season, wheat, barley, oats, rye, and peas, more particularly. The late corn and buckwheat, and some lesser grains and vegetables, have been materially injured by the recent frost; . . . but we have great occasion for thanksgiving to Him who giveth the increase, that He has blest our labors, so that with prudence we shall have a comfortable supply for ourselves, and our brethren on the way, who may be in need, until another harvest; but we feel the need of more laborers, for this place. We want men. Brethren, come from the States, from the nations, come! and help us to build and grow, until we can say, enough—the valleys of Ephraim are full.[3]

This was the 1849 general epistle of the Presidency of the Church. Incidentally, a later passage in the same document held out a lure that would have been hard to resist: "The health of the Saints in the valley is good, and it is so seldom that any one dies, we scarce recollect when such an event last occurred."

Naturally, such high-flown descriptions could give rise to disappointment and ridicule. As one newspaper editor put it, these descriptions "sometimes represented things that had not yet gone through the formality of taking place." Here is one traveler's account that is the opposite of boosterism:

> Take a large dry goods box, fill it half full of sand, and put in a few rough stones, throw in an armful of cactus and a thimbleful of water in one corner, put in a horned rattle snake, a horned toad, a lizard, a tarantula, a centipede, a scorpion, and a wild thistle, then take a bird's eye view of it, and you have in miniature a fair

description of the beautiful fertile Arizona, or at least the greater portion of it.[4]

There must have been immigrants to Utah who had similar disappointments. One is reminded, for example, of the little Jewish agricultural colony at Clarion, near Gunnison.[5] And Lynn Rosenvall has recently completed a valuable list of abandoned settlements, each of which must have left behind it an abundance of human heartache and disillusionment.[6]

As for overcoming dryness, getting water onto the dry land, this story has been considered before, although we have not found any single treatment that adequately recounts the complex story of dams, reservoirs, canals, and ditches as they appeared in valley after valley—a complex network of vessels and capillaries that meant life. Leonard Arrington and Dean May recently studied the Mormon role in irrigation technology and found that it was not quite as remarkable as it had once been thought, although in a different way—in the village organization and cooperative approach—it retains its significance.[7] Irrigation was a phenomenon not confined to Utah, as we all know, for the same life-death struggle was played out in Colorado, New Mexico, Arizona, Idaho, Wyoming, and elsewhere. In terms of the time periods mentioned earlier, we should notice that during the second and third periods three trends had an impact on irrigation: farms became larger; dry farming was introduced and expanded to include a substantial portion of Utah crops; and high-line canals were built to more efficiently bring larger areas under irrigation.

The discouragement that beset more than a few of the Utah settlers was in part a result of extravagant hopes. But it could also result from the simple facts of life on the farm. Diarists often did not choose to dwell on the routine of manual labor, but there are some exceptions. Let us take a few glimpses into the life of Joseph Beecroft, not a large landowner but the kind of small farmer who must have been typical of most of those who cultivated Utah's soil in the first and second phases. Entries from an 1869 diary show him pulling weeds, trading mules, suffering from sweltering days and nights, repairing the kitchen, chinking the logs on the house, threshing wheat, weighing and

pouring molasses, and performing countless other chores. It
was a team enterprise with wife and children pitching in. And
often in the background, although mentioned in few diaries,
were the adverse elements. "We all have prickly heat," Beecroft
wrote. "We can do no work in the heat of the day." Or on
another occasion: "For days we have had much wind which has
made it unpleasant working out of doors."[8] We could follow
farmer Beecroft through much more of his routine—what he
calls his "rounds" of work—but perhaps this gives the idea of
the kind of drudgery that was involved, the close dependence on
weather conditions, the small amounts produced, the possibilities of discouragement.

Part of the problem, especially during those first years in the
new territory, was simply to find out what would grow and what
would not. When Brigham Young arrived on 24 July 1847, he
found the advanced party already engaged in plowing and
planting potatoes. Within the next week 53 acres were plowed
and several acres were planted with buckwheat, corn, oats,
beans, and other garden seeds. Soon some plants were beginning to show above the ground. A year later Parley P. Pratt
described a bounteous harvest consisting of lettuce, radishes,
"beets, onions, peas, beans, cucumbers, melons, squashes and
almost all kinds of vegetables, as well as corn, oats, rye and
wheat."[9]

Edward Hunter, in reporting to the American Pomological
Society on the state of fruit in the valley in 1855, had both
successes and failures to report. Peaches were doing very well, at
least eighteen varieties having been named and catalogued.
Many melons were growing, including watermelons weighing
50 to 60 pounds. Apple and apricot trees had been bearing fruit
for two or three years, but plum and cherry trees were producing
little worthy of notice, and no pear trees were bearing as yet.
Quite a variety of strawberries and grapes was available, but few
gooseberries and only wild currants—the ones brought in from
the States having been destroyed by grasshoppers.[10]

Several visitors to Utah in the 1850s seemed impressed with
the agricultural productivity and variety they saw. Some idea of
the extent and variety of fruit and vegetables growing in Utah by

1860 is evident from Richard Burton's comments upon his visit:

> Pomology is carefully cultivated; about one hundred varieties of apples have been imported, and of these ninety-one are found to thrive as seedlings. . . . Besides grapes and apples, there were walnuts, apricots and quinces, cherries and plums, currants, raspberries and gooseberries. The principal vegetables were the Irish and the sweet potatoes, squashes, peas—excellent—cabbages, beets, cauliflowers, lettuce, and broccoli; a little rhubarb is cultivated, but it requires too much expensive sugar for general use, and white celery has lately been introduced.[11]

And in visiting Wilford Woodruff's garden, Burton noted the presence of

> . . . apricots from Malta, the Hooker strawberries, here worth $5 the plant, plum-trees from Kew Gardens, French and California grapes, wild plum and buffalo berry, black currants, peaches and apples. . . . The kitchen garden contained rhubarb, peas, potatoes, Irish and sweet, asparagus, white and yellow carrots, cabbages, and beets.[12]

Isolated as they were, the Mormon pioneers had to rely on several methods to bring into the territory the many varieties of crops, vegetables, and fruits they would need to sustain their ever-growing population. Some seeds were brought with companies as they came, of course, but not always with official approval. One determined sister, Margaret Tharuber Shaw, found some currants while crossing the plains in 1852 and, despite threats and warnings from the captain, she let the company go on without her while she gathered currants in her apron. She trudged into camp on foot the next night, strung her currants, and looped the thread across the top of the covered wagon to dry. Currant bushes from these seeds are said to have been distributed far and wide in Utah.[13]

Some members of the Mormon Battalion brought various seeds and grain with them upon their return from California. Club-head wheat and the California pea were two such imports. Daniel Tyler left six quarts of his California peas with Seely Owens to raise on shares with the two men planning to split the proceeds. In the first year or two, however, these were often used for subsistence rather than providing seed for later crops.[14]

Attempts were made in the first few years of settlement to send small trees and plants across the plains—a more difficult undertaking than simply sending seeds. David Sessions successfully sent several fruit trees to his parents—apple, peach, apricot, plum, and pear, along with some berry bushes—until in 1850 he came to the valley himself. He would wrap them in burlap in small bundles, tie them on the wagons of departing companies and pay the drivers to pour water on them at each watering place.[15] Lorenzo Dow Young was another who tried to bring growing trees across the plains in their own soil during those early years. He got several varieties through, but eventually all but one apple tree was lost.[16]

The establishment of commercial nurseries in Utah actually began very early. Thomas H. Woodbury is said to have established the Pioneer Nurseries in Salt Lake City as far back as 1850.[17] Luther S. Hemenway was probably another of the first men to establish a nursery in Salt Lake City. He arrived in October of 1853 and began his nursery soon after, teaching his daughters to graft and bud the trees. By 1855 he had fourteen thousand apple and peach trees ready for the market. Two years later he ran an ad in the *Deseret News* indicating that he had nine varieties of apple trees, two thousand currant bushes, and five thousand peach, plum and apricot trees. C. H. Oliphant also started a nursery about 1853 or 1854 that was thriving within a year or two. Even President Heber C. Kimball marketed five thousand peach trees in 1857.[18]

Individuals interested in promoting the growth of agriculture or horticulture in the territory might receive official blessings or callings from Church authorities to assist in their professional endeavors. C. H. Oliphant reported that

> Some time in the Spring of 1856, Pres't. Young put his hands on my head and set me apart to make my calling the growing of trees, shrubs, and etc. and the introducing of everything of this kind that is good among the Saints in Utah, and to this end he blessed me.[19]

When he was preparing to move to the valley in 1860, Joseph E. Johnson sent at least one wagon (and possibly three) loaded with seeds, trees, and various plant material in a wagon train ahead of him. One of his wives, Eliza, was sent along to care for the material, unloading the bales and watering them each night. Joseph brought more plants and trees when he followed in 1861.[20] The mail was probably the most common method for receiving new varieties of seeds. The correspondence of John D. Oakley (1868-72) reveals a thriving communication with seed companies, requesting such items as strap turnip, mustard, early salmon radish, netted citron melon, yellow Danvers onion, and quince. C. H. Oliphant received many fruit seeds and cuttings from friends in San Jose and San Bernardino. He even ordered from companies as far distant as New York, but sometimes items went astray. On one occasion, as he describes it,

> I sent to Ellwanger and Barry of Rochester for cuttings and small trees. They put me up about 40 dollars worth. There was then an express across the Plains; by this I directed it to be sent. By a strange fatality the parcel went via California. I traced this to San Francisco and there I lost all track of it.[22]

Some individuals brought back seeds from their visits to foreign lands. Robert Skelton, returning from a mission to India in 1853, brought the first Paradise tree seeds with him to Tooele.[22] Joseph Toronto made a visit to his homeland in Italy in 1875. When he returned two years later he brought from Sicily "roots of fig trees, lemons, oranges, English walnuts, bamboo and cane." Although only a few grew, a fig tree, walnut tree, and a bamboo plant all did quite well.[23]

Many new varieties of seeds, plants, and fruit were developed by experimentation in the territory as well as imported from outside. Israel Barlow and a Brother Tuttle in the West Bountiful area were said to have budded two or three kinds of fruit on one tree—for greater variety and for the novelty of it.[24] Luther S. Hemenway claimed to have produced one hundred fifty varieties of potato by 1862 and exhibited at that year's territorial fair the seven varieties he considered equal in quality to and more productive than the generally used Meshanic.[25]

Not only individuals but a number of organizations and societies disseminated information in Utah. Most prominent among these societies was the Deseret Agricultural and Manufacturing Society.[26] Organized originally in September of 1855 as the Deseret Horticultural Society, it was incorporated by the Utah Legislature that winter as the Deseret Agricultural and

Manufacturing Society. With Wilford Woodruff as president, along with other high Church leaders and prominent horticulturists on the board of directors, the society held meetings at which fruit was displayed and possibilities for different species were discussed. Later the organization concerned itself with all types of growing and manufacturing activities.

The Deseret Agricultural and Manufacturing Society established an experimental farm, named Deseret Gardens, at the mouth of Emigration Canyon. A gardener hired to work the farm on shares reported frequently to the board on the success of his crops. Some crops during the first ten years of operation were cotton, sorghum, tobacco, flax, grapes, peaches, apples, pears, potatoes, and sugar cane.[27] The black Imphee cane seed, for example, was tried in 1863 and 1864 but found to require too long a season to mature. The society, after experimenting with Hemenway's three most valuable potato varieties in 1866, found them not very flavorable, while recognizing that in other soils the result might be different.[28]

The society was very active in securing seeds. A motion at the 16 April 1865 meeting to allot $200 to "send for seeds to the States" was not unusual.[29] The society requested samples from the Agricultural Commissioner at Washington as well. For example, in 1865 they asked for some indigo seed they hoped to send to the south for possible cultivation.[30] The society looked far and wide in its attempts to procure seeds of various types— as can be seen by this entry in the minutes of 3 April 1864:

> Received from Col. Warren, Ed., of the Cal. Farmer 3 lbs. onion seed sent for March 15, also the following: From Japan—extra sized chestnuts; beans; peas; squash; curious nuts; Highland rice; chestnuts. From Batavia—Fine flowering trees; Accacia; tree cotton; Quassi; ornamental tree; beautiful yellow flowers; very rare seeds from Fayal and Batavia. From England—A new climbing bean, bright flowers; Sugar Beet No. 1; fine Hubbard squash; green flesh melon; Apple pie melon; Ponciana Regia (one of the most beautiful trees known); Pure Sea Island-Upland Cotton; North Carolina Cotton; Alabama Tobacco seed; Maryland Tobacco.[31]

This society acted as something of a clearing house for agricultural matters in the territory. It sent out forms and received back reports from various settlements and counties about their crops. The reports indicated what crops and trees were being raised, how large the acreage and yield were, the state of the produce, the weather, yearly comparisons, and other such information by which the society could keep track of progress in the territory as a whole. The society furnished the Agricultural Bureau in Washington with the names of correspondents for each county and helped facilitate communication both within the territory and with other states and horticultural organizations. It also distributed a great deal of reading material through the territory.

The society provided help and advice to communities not only about planting and growing but also about the formation of local organizations. Upon receiving a communication from Grantsville asking "sundrie questions about organization of Farmers Club," the secretary was directed to answer "according to answers proposed by the Board." Such questions and responses had become routine.

One of the most visible activities of the society was the annual territorial fair—a showcase to display and reward the best efforts of Utah producers in a number of categories. Prizes were awarded and premiums for all categories publicized widely as incentives for participation. The first exhibit in 1856 offered 12 silver medals, 205 diplomas and $880 in cash awards.

The society found it valuable to make use of Church channels to aid in their efforts as well. For example, a list of "missionaries" was drawn up who were assigned to visit the various wards on a designated Sunday and "advocate the interests of the Society and Fair."[32] On another occasion three members of the Board of Directors were appointed to attend the bishops' meeting and "lay the interests of the Society before the Bishops and ask their influence in their respective wards to make the Fair a success."

The Deseret Agricultural and Manufacturing Society was only one of the many groups in the territory devoted to the promotion of agriculture and related fields. Local groups sprang up in almost every community. Some were offshoots of the parent society, carrying the same name. Others were independent, and some communities had more than one group. In 1872, according to the minute book of the Salt Lake City society, agricultural societies existed at American Fork, Beaver City, Brigham City, Cedar City, Ephraim, Fairview, Farmington, Gunnison, Heber City, Meadow Creek, Moroni, Mount Pleasant, Manti, Nephi, Ogden, Parowan, Payson, Provo, Santaquin, Smithfield, Spanish Fork, St. George, Toquerville, Virgin City, and Washington.[33] There may have been others that escaped the attention of the secretary.

Most of these groups were teaching vehicles as well as organizations for cooperation in procuring the best seeds and varieties of plants. Luther S. Hemenway, chairman of the Gardener's Club of Deseret (formed by 1859), gave lectures and shared his expertise with others. Joseph E. Johnson not only had an outstanding garden and greenhouse for display in St. George but also taught what he had learned at the local Gardener's Club, which he was instrumental in founding.

The printed word was an additional channel used to spread information and suggestions for improving agriculture in Utah. Early newspapers are full of national information, local treatises, letters asking questions—and then hints and answers. Some issues of the *Deseret News* almost resemble an agricultural newspaper. There were, in addition, specialized newspapers and periodicals devoted to agriculture, such as *The Farmer's Oracle*, edited in 1863 and 1864 by Joseph E. Johnson from Spring Lake Villa.[34]

In the activity of sending for seeds or plants, trying them out, and disseminating knowledge about them, there are many unsung heroes in the generation extending from 1847 to the 1870s. In addition to Hemenway and Johnson, this group included William C. Staines, Louis Bertrand, Albert Carrington, and many others. Probably the important thing to recognize is that just about every farmer—or city dweller with an acreage—would be interested in knowing what to plant, when to plant, what kind of soil was needed, how much water to use, kinds and amounts of fertilizer, and other similar information. Then there was the question of enemies: insects, blight, and different diseases. What could be done about them?

Such subjects were discussed among individuals, within families, at the fairs, in the agricultural societies, and interminably in the pages of Utah's many newspapers. Subscribers to the *Deseret News*, the St. George *Union*, the Davis County *Clipper*, and scores of other newspapers could almost always find information about new species, recommendations on planting, and the all-important market and weather information.

By the closing decade of the century, Utah farmers were able to benefit from genuinely professional help. Most impressive were the bulletins published during the 1890s by the Utah Agricultural Experiment Station, which appeared several times per year. Among others during that decade were bulletins on plowing, watering horses, proper feed for horses, proper amount of water for irrigating potatoes, grass-fed pigs versus nongrass-fed pigs, time for harvesting lucerne, and the relative value of corn and oats for horses.[35] Obviously, such pamphlets would be of great interest to the practicing farmer.

While Utah farmers were learning what would grow and what they could profitably sell, they were also taking advantage of improved farm machinery. The starting point was low. The first plows in 1847 were made by hammering the metal wagon rims that had come across the plains into a different configuration. In 1864 a little handwritten newspaper from St. George contained the following:

> Our principal interest is that of Agriculture, and yet a great lack of judgement is exhibited by our farmers in not providing themselves with the proper implements of husbandry. I doubt if there is a half dozen plows in St. George that is worth using. The writer of this article has had occasion to use his neighbors' plows, and he being partial to good plows directed his efforts to the obtaining of such a one, but strange to tell, he was unable to find a plow fit for use. Many persons who profess to be farmers have no plows at all. There is also a great scarcity of other tools necessary for the faithful and successful cultivation of the soil.
>
> Is there the first cotton scraper in Washington County? We have not seen or heard of one. But we can more easily enumerate the tools owned and used by our farmers, than name those, that are indispensible, which our farmers have failed to procure. About one worthless turning plow, out of repair, to every two families, is a fair estimate. One bull tongue to every thirty families; one shovel

plow to every hundred families and there is a few draggs, cultivators and harrows, but of a very trifling character. These comprise the list of tools, to which horse power is applied in the cultivation of the crops. The smaller tools such as hoes, shovels, spades, axes & c. are more general, yet much too scarce; and many of them of an inferior quality. The surplus labor with a good tool over and above that which could be done with a poor one, will often pay for itself in a week, frequently in less time—yet many persons' idea of economy induces them to retain their poor worn out articles year after year rather than invest a few dollars for a serviceable one. As strange as it may seem the fruits of this thriftless policy is exhibited all around.[36]

Some improved equipment found its way to Utah fairly quickly after being introduced on the national scene, but the distribution was uneven and sometimes slow.

Although reapers were developed by the 1830s, they were not used extensively until about 1850. A McCormick reaper and mower was exhibited at Farmington as early as 1856. From the enthusiastic newspaper reports, this may have been the first view of such a machine in Utah. One Davis County farmer said he was through with cradling if he could get a reaper to cut his grain and asked, "Why have we been without them so long? I hope that some of our principal farmers and capitalists will send and procure a supply for the Territory."[37] Previous to this time, and indeed for some time afterwards in many areas, the primitive sickle and slightly improved cradle were the standard implements available for harvesting crops in Utah.

It took until the 1870s for the later improved harvesting devices to make their appearance in Utah. St. George had at least two Wood mowing machines in 1874, an Osborne self-rake harvester in 1876, and a self-binder by 1878, followed by several more of these handy machines through the next two decades. In 1878 the McCormick self-binder was on exhibit in Kaysville and competed against a Wood self-binding harvester and an Osborne machine in an exhibition contest, the results of which were inconclusive as each machine had its defenders.[38] The one thing all agreed upon was that these machines were decidedly more efficient than their predecessors. Their main appeal was the binding mechanism, as the twelve acres per day which they harvested was no more than that cut by the 1856 machines.

The threshing machine was the other improvement most in evidence in Utah, appearing even in the earliest years. Grain-threshing machines devised to replace the standard flailing by hand were in use in the United States as early as 1825 but were not used extensively until around 1840. One early type was operated by horsepower on a treadmill, a sweep horsepower device in which the horses made a huge circle to operate the mechanism.

In August of 1848 it was reported that "Brother Leffingwell has built a threshing machine and fanning mill, on City Creek, that will treat and clean 200 bushels per day."[39] Christopher Layton related in his autobiography that when he arrived in Salt Lake in September of 1852 "I had brought with me a new threshing machine, one of the first, if not the very first, in Utah."[40] Perhaps this was a new type, for in the Fifth General Epistle of 7 April 1851, the First Presidency noted that

> Two or three threshing machines have been in successful operation in our valley, the past fall and winter, which have saved the labor of many hundred days.[41]

But while the numbers of threshers increased, there were some problems connected with their operation. The *Deseret News* of 23 July 1856 noted the following:

> Thrashing machines, some with separators, and two or more with fans, are becoming quite plenty.
> But it appears to be very difficult to arrange a machine that thrashes well in the States, so that it will thrash equally well with different varieties, qualities and conditions of grain to be found here. Even with moveable concaves and the best of feeding, it does happen that a machine either fails to thrash clean, or breaks the kernel. Much study and pains have been expended to avoid these objections, and it is presumable that the well known skill of our mechanics and others will be able to overcome the difficulty, and that machines will be so constructed as to thrash clean and whole.

Horsepowered imported threshers were appearing in places such as Mendon and St. George by the early and mid-1860s. Communities that could not afford or chose not to buy manufactured threshers could make their own. A threshing machine is said to have been made in Manti by local blacksmiths and carpenters in the early 1860s. Both it and the accompanying fanner were "company owned" and shared as needed.[42] Fewer threshers were needed than harvesters, since it was more feasible to share the use and not every farmer needed his own. Mendon had a Pitt thresher and separator—which winnowed the grain also—as early as 1865. The community acquired improved separators in the 1880s that operated by horse power until 1892, when steam power replaced the horses.

> Throngs of people turned out to see the harnessed steam, which so peacefully and quietly performed its task as the first engineer, George Sanders, proudly demonstrated his perfect control over the untiring iron horse.
>
> They gazed upon it with amazement and suspicion by some who predicted "She'd blow up," and they kept their distance. But she continued to keep the wheels of the old Advance rolling regardless of their crowding and trying to stall.[43]

Although combines were developed early in the 1800s and were used in California as early as 1854 with extensive use in the 1870s and 1880s, they do not seem to have made an appearance in Utah before the early 1900s.

VALUE OF FARM MACHINERY

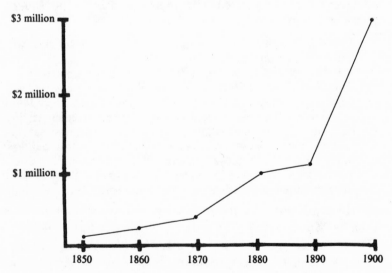

Source: *12th U.S. Census, 1900*, vol. 5, 1, pp. 698-99.

Neff, quoting census figures that placed a value of $84,288 on Utah farming implements and machinery in 1850 and $242,889 in 1860, claimed that "Comparative data reveals that Utah was leading all the territories in the utilization of modern machinery.[44] By 1878 farm machinery business certainly seemed to be booming in Cache Valley. One letter to the *Deseret News* reported that in that county alone there were sixty threshing machines and two thousand harvesters and reapers.[45] But it must be remembered that the spread of these new machines was uneven and the extent of their use in Utah far from uniform. The graph on the preceeding page gives some idea of the increase in farm machinery.

Incidentally, much of what has already been discussed came together in the effort to solve one of the greatest problems to early Utah agriculture—the grasshopper threat. It was not only in that great "cricket" invasion of 1848 we are so familiar with but in many additional years also—sometimes several in succession—that the "pestiferous ironclads" came and wiped out part or all of the crops. The finest seeds in the world were of no use if the insects were able to destroy the new plants before they could mature. The grasshoppers could mean famine and economic ruin. The early Utah settlers tried to find out what they could on the subject, applied technology to the invention of grasshopper machines, and organized programs to resist them. The dissemination of grasshopper information, drawn from national publications as well as local recommendations, took place in the same societies, church meetings, and periodicals that were used for disseminating information about agriculture in general.[46]

Farming in Utah was steadily modernized through the decades leading toward statehood. In what ways did the fact that this was in large measure a Mormon population affect the process? Did the Church slow down the modernization or speed it up? Discourage it or encourage it? And, to pose a more difficult question, did the changing face of Utah's agriculture in turn have any noticeable effect on the religion?

The influence of the LDS Church seems to have been entirely positive, a stimulus to the modernization we have been describing. This is apparent on two levels, practical and ideological. To begin with a fact so obvious that it is easy to overlook, it was Mormonism that brought most of these people to Utah where they would have to farm to a greater or lesser degree—many of them coming from the factories of Manchester and the urban centers of the East. And it was the Church that continued to fling out settlements that provided fresh inducements and opportunities for the faithful to stake claims, sink their plows into the soil, and draw sustenance from the land. Admittedly, some of this would have happened anyway, but it was Mormonism that provided the lure and imposed the pattern of agricultural settlements.

Then, too, it was the Church that provided several of the channels for disseminating information about methods of farming, what seeds to plant, and marketing possibilities. Admittedly, there were secular channels—government bulletins, newspapers, fairs, and many agricultural societies—that could have done the job in the absence of the Church, as of course they did in other parts of the United States. But given the nature of Utah society, it is not surprising that Church newspapers and Church meetings were the forum for disseminating much of the information.

> I do not wish to hear again any of the leaders of Israel complain that there is not any pure sugar-cane seed, flaxseed, cotton seed, &c., in the country, but I wish them to be fully informed as to where pure seeds of all kinds can be had, and as to what is going on among the people in every part of each Ward or district.[47]

This advice from Brigham Young in 1862 is but one example among many of the involvement of Church officials in the details of improving agriculture.

Ideologically, a cluster of Mormon ideas proved encouraging to agriculture in general and to whatever modernizing improvements could be made. To make the desert blossom as the rose—this was their self-proclaimed goal as they settled the Great Basin. Such an enterprise was a holy one, sanctioned and blessed by the God of Heaven. Listen to William C. Staines in his comments to the first public meeting of the Deseret Horticultural Society in 1855:

Many wondered when they came here if fruit could be raised. I believed it could be raised and went to work accordingly. . . . Some argue that it is too expensive to fence and raise fruit, but it is my business to decorate and beautify Zion—it is part of my religion, as much as going to meetings and praying and singing.[48]

This attitude was common. Providing a religious sanction for the activity of farming and an implicit assurance of success, in the long run if not necessarily in the short run, the Mormon religion should be thought of as not exclusively rural in its emphasis but nevertheless as showing a repeated bias in favor of agricultural activity and the rural life, in the nineteenth century at least.

To bring this point into sharper focus it will be helpful to consider how Mormon leaders spoke of agriculture by comparison to rival occupations and modes of life. We do not wish to overstate this point because in fact manufacture continued to expand throughout the period of territorial Utah, and the urban centers—mainly Salt Lake City and Ogden—continued to grow. But even urban life in such cities was not far removed from the garden soil, chicken coop, barns, and pastures necessary for the animals almost every family possessed.[49] And the manufacture, such as it was, could in large measure be seen as an effort to preserve the self-sufficiency of the Great Basin by having coal, iron, sugar, and textiles. What William Blake called the "dark Satanic mills" of England's factory towns were far from a practical possibility in Utah during its first half-century of white population.

Against this backdrop the inherited preference for agriculture as a mode of life was first dramatized when some Mormons expressed an interest in going off to the mines of California. The attraction of mining became even more immediate with the great expansion of such activity in Utah after the coming of the railroad. In both situations, if we interpret the evidence correctly, the attitude of Church leaders was not quite a total prohibition. Leonard Arrington, in his *Great Basin Kingdom*, has explained the policy that was hammered out in the 1850s and 1860s.[50] In time the Church itself and some Church leaders invested in mining, but there is no mistaking their general attitude about what was preferable and wholesome for the membership at large. "We have all the time prayed that the Lord would shut up the mines," said Apostle Erastus Snow. "It is better for us to live in peace and good order, and to raise wheat, corn, potatoes, and fruit, than to suffer the evils of a mining life."[51]

Lest such statements be seen as temporary, short-sighted expressions that would quickly dissolve in the actual diversified economic development of the territory, it is valuable to notice at the end of the century, and even beyond, repeated injunctions from Church leaders encouraging young people to stay on the farm, to stay away from the cities, to seek practical education—all Mormon variations of the national "farm life movement" that burgeoned in the early twentieth century.[52] Only reluctantly did Church leaders recognize that more and more of their people, eventually a majority, would be city dwellers rather than farmers. And even then, if we are not mistaken, valiant efforts were made to retain what they perceived as the purity, wholesomeness, hard work, independence, and self-sufficiency of the farm.

But if such a pronounced pro-agricultural bias, along with the practical needs of providing the necessities of life in a new area, inclined Mormonism to encourage agriculture, what does this imply for the modernization of agriculture we have been examining here? It is quite possible to prefer or even require a rural tempo of life on religious grounds—one thinks of the Hutterites or Amish—without showing receptivity to new-fangled devices. Indeed, if the old-fashioned farm provides the right setting for human relations, physical and moral de-velopment, and a sense of dependency on the Creator, it can be convincingly argued that the introduction of machinery—leading eventually to commercial agriculture and the demise of the family farm—is as much a threat as the urbanization of which it is the counterpart.

Although such hostility to innovation and technology might seemingly have been a possibility, it was simply not part of the Mormon ideology. "The morning breaks, the shadows flee, the clouds of error disappear," wrote Apostle Parley P. Pratt in one of the earliest and most popular Mormon hymns. And over and over again the dawning sun was interpreted to mean not only the restored gospel but also other kinds of progress, most obviously and oftmentioned improved transportation by steam and rail and accelerated communication by telegraph. Here is a statement by Apostle Orson Pratt in 1873:

> The Lord for a score or two of years has been working in order to establish among men, facilities for conveying knowledge to the uttermost corners of the earth. Within the memory of many now living, the discovery of the electric telegraph has been made, by means of which news of the doings of men in any country can be sent round the earth in less than twenty-four hours. . . . The great object which the Lord had in view when this great invention or discovery was brought forth, was to enable knowledge to be sent from the mountain tops, from the midst of Zion, when his glory should begin to be manifested in the midst of his people in the latter days.[53]

A new invention in technology, in other words, had a divine purpose—thus making it not only permissible to Mormons but emphatically part of the arsenal with which God was equipping them to accomplish His purposes. This was said in dramatic terms of the railroad, seen as the great highway of Biblical prophecy that would enable the Saints to gather from all corners of the globe.[54]

Of course, simple cost-accounting might have been sufficient to bring threshing machines, reapers, and the like to Mormon country, but when there was already present a predisposing mind set recognizing in technology a heaven-sent help, the resulting rapid reception of improved, mechanized agriculture was inevitable. The Latter-day Saints were to make the desert blossom as the rose. To till the soil in the laborious, traditional manner of some Indian tribes—using gourds to bring small amounts of water onto small tracts of ground and pounding the corn by hand—would scarcely accomplish the purpose. In the Mormons' view, God had provided them with information about scientific farming (the whole idea of which was not very old in the mid-nineteenth century), surveyors and techniques by which irrigation could be a large-scale, effective means of transforming arid wastes into irrigated fields, and various

channels by which information could be disseminated about
honey bees, sheep, dairy cattle, and all kinds of seeds. Not
surprisingly, the McCormick reaper and the later threshing
machines were seen as part of the same convergence of
techniques and circumstances that would allow the miraculous
creation of Zion in the West.

Whatever the combination of reasons, Utah's agriculture
experienced a remarkable transition from the original settlement by the end of the century. It was a complex story, of which
we have mentioned only a part. The continued influx of
immigrants, the opening up of new settlements, the establishment of a network of roads and railroads linking farms to
markets, the development of an export trade of impressive
dimensions—all these were part of the change.[55] Pride in
achievement was noted quite early—in the various territorial
fairs, in the jubilee celebration of 1880, and in all kinds of
boosting literature published in periodicals and pamphlets. If
Charles S. Peterson is right in his thesis that the Americanization of Utah's agriculture occurred mainly in the decade of
the 1890s, it should be recognized that all the major trends had
started earlier and that dramatic gains already had been made.[56]
In 1893, at the great World's Columbian Exposition, Utah
exhibited an ambitious display of agriculture, including an
elaborate relief map of an irrigated valley that even modern
museum personnel could admire. In summarizing Utah's
relative showing, the official report stated:

> In the Agricultural Department Utah occupied a choice position.
> Our pavilion . . . was not so elaborately decorated as the pavilions
> of some of the neighboring states, but in products of the soil
> shown we acknowledged no superior. We could not rival Iowa or
> Illinois in corn, nor Louisiana or Kentucky in sugar cane or
> tobacco, but take the average of the products of the soil from the
> States and Utah equaled and outstripped them. Our test applied,
> and showed a marked superiority over those from any other State.
> It was clearly demonstrated that Utah yields more wealth from the
> soil per capita, counting only the farming population, than any
> other State.[57]

Such forgivable pride continued throughout the decade and
beyond.

We have concentrated on one aspect of a large development, that which to us seems the major theme of the nineteenth century in Utah's agriculture. Was there any intimation, we might ask in conclusion, of that counter theme, the idea of the "machine in the garden," the ominous fear that technology would bring in its train not blessings but problems and ugliness? Was there any suggestion that agricultural technology might end the family farm or, by extension, that industrial technology could bring a laboring proletariat, slums, crime, and pollution? Not really, insofar as we have been able to tell. The Mormons, like other Americans of the past century, were riding the wave of supreme confidence in something called progress, which the Latter-day Saints conveniently lined up to their own interpretation of the religious significance of time. If there was some deepening awareness of complexity, the loud hurrahs and fireworks of the celebration of statehood easily drowned out any quiet wonderings.

Notes

1. In addition to several theses, the following published works are of value: Wain Sutton, ed., *Utah: A Centennial History* (New York: Lewis Historical Publishing Co., 1949); Charles S. Peterson, "The 'Americanization' of Utah's Agriculture," *Utah Historical Quarterly* 42 (1974): 108-25, which in a footnote surveys the published literature.

2. Daniel Boorstin, *The Americans: The National Experience* (New York: Random House, 1965), p. 126.

3. James R. Clark, ed., *Messages of the First Presidency*, 6 vols. (Salt Lake City: Bookcraft, 1965-75), 2:33.

4. *Deseret News*, 24 December 1862.

5. Everett L. Cooley, "Clarion, Utah, Jewish Colony in 'Zion,'" *Utah Historical Quarterly* 36 (1968): 113-31.

6. Lynn A. Rosenvall, "Defunct Mormon Settlements, 1830-1930," in Richard H. Jackson, ed., *The Mormon Role in the Settlement of the West*, Charles Redd Monographs in Western History, no. 9 (Provo, Utah: Brigham Young University Press, 1978).

7. Leonard J. Arrington and Dean L. May, "A Different Mode of Life: Irrigation and Society in Nineteenth-Century Utah," *Agricultural History* 49 (January 1975): 3-20.

8. Joseph Beecroft Diary, Archives of the Church of Jesus Christ of Latter-day Saints, Salt Lake City (hereafter referred to as LDS Church Archives).

9. Journal History of the Church of Jesus Christ of Latter-day Saints, 10 August 1848, LDS Church Archives.

10. Edward Hunter to Marshall P. Wilder, 24 August 1855, quoted in *Heart Throbs of the West*, 12 vols. (Salt Lake City, Utah: Daughters of Utah Pioneers, 1947-51), 10:205-6 (hereafter referred to as *HTW*).

11. Richard Burton, *City of the Saints* (New York: Alfred A. Knopf, 1963), pp. 297-98.

12. Ibid., p. 401.

13. *HTW*, 10:185.

14. Daniel Tyler, *A Concise History of the Mormon Battalion in the Mexican War, 1846-47* (Chicago: Rio Grande Press, 1964), pp. 318-19.

15. *HTW*, 10:212-13.

16. Ibid., 193.

17. Ibid., 209.

18. Ibid., 187.

19. Ibid., 194.

20. Ibid., 195-96.

21. C. H. Oliphant, Autobiography, p. 12., LDS Church Archives.

22. *HTW*, 10:230.

23. Ibid., 220.

24. Ibid., 221.

25. Ibid., 188.

26. Leonard J. Arrington, "The Deseret Agricultural and Manufacturing Society in Pioneer Utah," *Utah Historical Quarterly* 24 (1956): 165-70.

27. Martha E. Gibbs, "The Utah State Fair," typescript, LDS Church Archives.

28. Deseret Agricultural and Manufacturing Society Minute Book, LDS Church Archives, pp. 41-42.

29. Ibid., 37.

30. Ibid., 30.

31. Ibid., 17.

32. Ibid., 26 September 1863.

33. Ibid., 3 August 1872, p. 103.

34. Rufus David Johnson, *J. E. J. Trail to Sundown: The Story of a Pioneer, Joseph Ellis Johnson* (Salt Lake City: Deseret News Press, n. d.), pp. 360-78.

35. These are samples of a hundred or more Utah Agricultural Experiment Station Bulletins, which we have examined at the University of Utah's Marriott Library, Salt Lake City.

36. *Veprecula*, St. George, Utah, 1864, manuscript newspaper, LDS Church Archives.

37. *Deseret News*, 16, 23 July 1856.

38. *Deseret News*, 3, 5 July 1878; *Salt Lake Tribune*, 4, 5 July 1878.

39. Journal History, 8 August 1848.

40. Myron W. McIntyre and Noel R. Barton, eds., *Christopher Layton* (Salt Lake City: privately published, 1966), p. 81.

41. James R. Clark, ed., *Messages of the First Presidency* 6 vols. (Salt Lake City: Bookcraft, 1965-1975), 2:65.

42. *HTW*, 4:401.

43. Ibid., 395.

44. Andrew Love Neff, *History of Utah, 1847-69* (Salt Lake City: Deseret News Press, 1940), p. 267.

45. *Deseret News Weekly*, 30 May 1877.

46. Davis Bitton and Linda P. Wilcox, "Pestiferous Ironclads: The Grasshopper Problem in Pioneer Utah," *Utah Historical Quarterly* 46 (Fall 1978): 336-55.

47. Brigham Young et al., *Journal of Discourses*, 26 vols. (London: Latter-day Saints' Book Depot, 1855-96), 10:34.

48. *HTW*, 10:207.

49. Lowry Nelson, *The Mormon Village: A Pattern and Technique of Land Settlement* (Salt Lake City: n. p., 1952); Richard V. Francaviglia, *The Mormon Landscape* (New York: AMS Press, 1978).

50. Leonard J. Arrington, *Great Basin Kingdom: An Economic History of the Latter-day Saints* (Cambridge, Mass.: Harvard University Press, 1958), chs. 2-7.

51. Journal History, 5 June 1870.

52. This theme is abundantly treated in *The Contributor*, the official Young Men's Mutual Improvement Association organ, during the years 1880-96, and in the early volumes of the *Improvement Era*. One example among many is Lewis Merrill, "Choosing an Occupation," *Improvement Era* 5 (January 1902): 212-16.

53. *Journal of Discourses*, 16:83.

54. Ibid.,12:271. But see William S. Adkins, "Anticipation of the Pacific Railroad in Mormon Utah, 1868-69," unpublished paper in our possession.

55. Some of these we have treated in Davis Bitton and Linda Wilcox, "Utah Farm Life in Relation to its National Setting, 1896-1916," unpublished report prepared for the Wheeler Historic Farm, Salt Lake City, in 1979, in our possession.

56. Charles S. Peterson, "The 'Americanization' of Utah's Agriculture."

57. *Utah at the World's Columbian Exposition* (n.p., 1894), p. 79.

Young Heber J. Grant:
Entrepreneur Extraordinary

Ronald W. Walker

If, as Gerald Nash suggests in the essay opening this volume, to understand the twentieth-century American West it is necessary to come to grips with its late nineteenth-century antecedents, the following essay by Ronald W. Walker, Senior Historical Associate, Joseph Fielding Smith Institute for Church History at Brigham Young University, should prove useful. During the period under consideration, Heber J. Grant, the subject of this study, was perhaps the foremost young entrepreneur of territorial Utah. As Dr. Walker points out, he was engaged in a wide range of business enterprises that included insurance companies, commercial establishments, livery and carrying, and banks.

Grant's story is that of a poor but well-connected young man with an enormous drive for success. He was willing to risk his health and assets in the hope of future wealth. His values were those we associate with Victorian America, and Dr. Walker is right in comparing him to Horatio Alger and Russell Conwell.

Beyond this, however, and in common with many other entrepreneurs of the period, his motives were not entirely selfish. His motivation, like Andrew Carnegie's, included building the community, and his patronage of the arts and private philanthropies and his commitment to his church were, if anything, greater than those of John D. Rockefeller.

Grant was an individual to be sure, but he also represented a select group of business entrepreneurs who could be found throughout the late nineteenth-century West. Most did not become prominent ecclesiastical leaders, but they often served the public in other ways through charitable organizations and ventures. Most important, the business organizations and philanthropic institutions these men organized and promoted have continued in the twentieth-century West. The Heber J. Grant Insurance Agency, Zion's Cooperative Mercantile Institution, and a host of other companies, many of which have passed through mergers and reorganizations, trace their origins to Grant's entrepreneurship.

When lecturing at the Harvard Law School, Justice Oliver Wendell Holmes told students they could do anything they wanted to in life, if only they wanted to hard enough. Later in a private aside he added, "But what I did not tell them was that they had to be born wanting to."[1]

Heber J. Grant was born wanting to be an entrepreneur. Young Heber consumed the commercial news of the *New York Weekly Ledger* as avidly as other boys might read the sports page. He and his close companion Heber Wells ventured into an ambitious but disastrous egg business (harried by neighborhood dogs and infested with the pip, the hens refused to lay). Heber even became a youthful employer. His keen eye and steady fingers won him a trove of marbles, and he used his winnings with Tom Sawyeresque skill. Less nimble companions were hired to cut wood, haul water, and do his other distasteful chores.[2]

Business ambitions boiled within the youth. "As a boy of seventeen, I dreamed in my mind about my future life," he later recalled. "I had never thought of holding a Church position; I had other plans." These he plotted with precision. First, he would master the tasks of business clerk and bookkeeper while still a teenager. Next, he resolved that by his twenty-first birthday he would have his own business concern. He projected that by the age of thirty he would be a director of Zion's Cooperative Mercantile Institution (ZCMI), Utah's largest wholesale and retail outlet. Other youthful plans were perhaps to found a local insurance company, preside over a Utah bank, or sit on the board of one of the transcontinental railroads.[3]

Why such a passion for business? One obvious answer is that it was a part of the times. During the last decades of the nineteenth century, the business of America *was* business. Daring entrepreneurs reaped fortunes by masterminding such exciting new industries as steel, oil, and electricity. These new captains of industry stamped their personalities upon their era and made private property, competitive enterprise, and corporate wealth appear as eternal verities. The cult of the self-made man arose. The Englishman Samuel Smiles and his American counterparts William Makepeace Thayer and Horatio Alger promised any determined, hard-working boy material success. As Alger penned in a couplet that included six of his 119 book titles:

> *Strive and Succeed*, the world's temptations flee—
> Be *Brave and Bold*, and *Strong and Steady* be.
> Go *Slow and Sure*, and prosper then you must—
> With *Fame and Fortune*, while you *Try and Trust*.[4]

Smiles's books on *Character*, *Thrift*, and *Self-Help* found their way into young Heber's hands, and the boy drank thirstily from the self-help draught. Local schools taught such precepts as duty, success, and moral truth from the widely used *Wilson* and *National* readers.[5] So indelible was the mark of these elementary school texts that Grant quoted from them the rest of his life. The devout Rachel Ivins Grant, Heber's widowed and subsequently divorced mother, hoped that her son might give himself to church service, but she by no means resisted the prevailing commercial climate. She herself came from a long line of Quaker merchants.

This new business spirit spilled into Utah's previously isolated valleys. From the twenty years following its founding, Utah had been a pioneer community. Survival, settlement, and the propagation of Mormon ideals were its concerns. But during the 1870s, the years when Heber Grant came of age, the territory began to enter the American mainstream. Across the tracks of the recently completed Union Pacific Railroad flowed products and ideas. Utah's mines began to prosper and Salt

Lake City acquired for the first time a rapidly growing commercial district. Many Mormon leaders caught the entrepreneuring fever, and their business activities impressed young Heber.

Among the enterprising young men who provided the boy with behavioral models was Joseph Elder, who owned a little frame grocery store a half block down Main Street from where the Grants lived. Heber, not yet six years old, spent hours at Elder's, endlessly listening and talking, being initiated into the mysteries of commerce. Another was the crusty and indefatigable Edwin Woolley, the Grants' Thirteenth Ward bishop and a man of many business endeavors. The bishop left such an impression that Heber later described him as "a good man, an honest man, a hard-working man—and a man I loved." But no acquaintance exercised a stronger business influence than the affable Alex Hawes. As the New York Life Insurance Company's agent for Salt Lake City and later for the Pacific Coast and England, Hawes typified the hard-working, principled, nineteenth-century business ideal. For six months Hawes roomed and boarded at the Grants, the beginning of a life-long bond between him and twelve-year-old Heber. Hawes recognized in the boy a budding talent of the first order, and for years afterward showered letters of fatherly encouragement upon his protege.[6]

Of course Heber's youthful experiences and contacts were not an alchemy that mysteriously and automatically produced an entrepreneur. Similar influences worked to no avail upon his boyhood friends. Tony (Anthony W.) Ivins, Dick (Richard W.) Young, Hebe (Heber M.) Wells, Fera (Feramorz) Young, Ort (Orson F.) Whitney, and Rud (Rudger) Clawson later would prove themselves to be remarkably talented, but none were compulsively drawn to the balance sheet or ledger like Heber.

Clearly there was something in Grant's personality that drew him to business. Whitney bemusedly remembered the boy as "a persevering sort of chap whose chief delight seemed to be in overcoming obstacles."[7] Despite a natural clumsiness, he determinedly set out to win the second base position with the Red Stockings, only to lose interest when the team gained the territorial championship. His fine penmanship came after classmates laughed at his blots and scribbles. Never a serious reader or scholar, he nevertheless had no rival when a concrete task or contest lay at hand, like the memorization of the Deseret Alphabet or Jaques's *Catechism*. After Bishop Woolley branded him a ne'er-do-well, he earnestly set out and won his approval.[8] "I confess there is something in being at the head," the compulsive achiever later admitted, "that has always favorably impressed me."[9]

Young Heber was developing other entrepreneurial virtues. His towering ambitions spoke loudly of his outward optimism and cocksureness. Such traits were later readily diagnosed by the celebrated and perceptive phrenologist Henry Fowler, who told the young man to reduce his "bump of hope" by half and be satisfied. Moreover he found that he could not "help working and that in a hurry." Upon securing his first office job at fifteen, he quickly mastered his tasks and asked for more. Four years later he almost resigned because of nothing to do. The young man in fact worked nights to complete his duties and was rewarded by his grateful employer with a $100 bonus for industry. "I did it," he explained without sensing there was anything unusual in his behavior, "because... I did not like to sit around idle."[10]

He learned self-reliance early, literally at his mother's knee. Despite her stately charm, Rachel Grant had not married until her middle thirties, only to be widowed when her only son was nine days old. The death of her husband, Jedediah Morgan Grant, and her unsuccessful remarriage to his dissolute brother, George D., left her impoverished. Young Heber recalled blustery nights with no fire in the hearth, months with no shoes, never more than a single homemade outfit of homespun at a time, and, except for an adequate supply of bread, a meagre fare that allowed only a pound of butter and four pounds of sugar for the entire year.[11] Although Rachel's education, personality, and intelligence placed her among Deseret's "first ladies," sewing became her means of avoiding charity. "I sat on the floor at night until midnight," Heber remembered, "and pumped the sewing machine to relieve her tired limbs."[12] The machine's constantly moving treadles became a symbol of the Grant's stubborn independence.

"A man who has been the indisputable favorite of his mother," theorized Freud, "keeps for life the feeling of conqueror, the confidence of success which often induces real success." Indeed there grew between mother and son a special bond that permanently etched a spirit of independence upon Heber's .character. On the one hand she indulged him, an advantage the boy later regretted exploiting. "Being both son and daughter to my mother," he remarked, "I suppose I may have been partially spoiled in the raising."[13] But on the other hand, she showered upon him her adult interests and high expectations. She never doubted that the boy's destiny would exceed his father's, who had served as mayor of the city and as Brigham Young's counselor. Her light discipline and heavy anticipations encouraged Heber to experiment—to raise chickens and to hire other boys with marbles. The consequence was a growing sense of mastery, a feeling that he could and should get things done.

To help his mother, the boy, then fourteen, worked twenty straight Saturdays at fifty cents a day to earn the ten dollars required to insure her modest home. Although Bishop Woolley protested that Widow Grant's many friends would quickly rebuild her home in case of a disaster, Heber replied that the Grants could do without such help. "I don't care to live in a house built by charity," he said. "I would be a little pauper, living in a house not knowing who furnished the money to build it, and therefore not being able to pay it back."[14]

Such fierce independence bred within Heber a resilience to popular opinion. "When certain people start to say kind things about me," he confided many years later, "I say, 'Heber Grant, what's the matter with you? If you were doing your duty that man wouldn't say good things about you.'"[15] His willingness to defend an unpopular position had taken root early. While reading the Book of Mormon at age fifteen, he strongly identified with the outspoken Nephi who often preached against the popular grain. The Nephite prophet became his hero, more influential in his life, he admitted, "than . . . any other character in ancient history, sacred or profane—save only the Redeemer of the world."[16]

The Book of Mormon was only one part of Mormonism's impact upon Heber. "As a boy he was inclined always to religion," recalled his intimate boyhood friend Richard Young. There was no wonder in this. Widow Grant had nourished him from infancy upon Mormonism's milk. Some of his earliest memories were of "going to meeting" to hear Brother Brigham. As a boy he proudly sat next to Bishop Woolley in the Thirteenth Ward meetinghouse to time speakers and meetings. When healthy and in town, the youth never missed attending General Conference. Nor could he remember an instance of playing Sabbath baseball. At fifteen he was ordained an Elder, several years later was chosen a Seventy, and at nineteen was called as a counselor in the first ward Mutual Improvement Association ever organized. As a young man he was careful with his tithing and donations. "He lives his religion," Richard Young reported, "but is seldom able to warm himself unto enthusiasm over a principle; his love is a practical, everyday, common-sense devotion to principles which from their superiority to all others, he chooses to believe are divine."[17]

More than supplying the young man with a system of religious ethics, Mormonism gave purpose and energy to his life. While not having an intellectual's appreciation for his religion, with its promises of human worth and a divinely ordered world, he nevertheless felt the empowering spirit of his faith. The sermons in the Tabernacle taught him that Mormons were a special people with a special mission. Thus the character of Nephi appealed to Grant not simply because of his outspokenness, but also because of his sense of mission—"his faith, his determination, his spirit to do the will of God."[18] Grant became such a disciple himself, possessed with the enormous energy given to those who are confident of their providential duty and destiny.

In summary, a modern behaviorist might use Grant as a case study of an innovative or entrepreneurial personality. Here was a bright boy with the deep needs of an achiever. Buoyant, self-confident, industrious, self-reliant, and tough-minded, he had acquired these entrepreneurial traits in a classic, textbook manner. He was the only child of a mature woman who had dominated him with loving indulgence and high standards. Heber's father figures—Joe Elder, Bishop Woolley, Alex Hawes, and Erastus Snow, an Apostle who took an unusual interest in the boy—supplied the quiet, pliant paternal influence that usually characterizes an innovator's childhood. Like most contemporary entrepreneurs, Grant rose from the urban middle class—if not in wealth, certainly in values and status. And as was also true of them, his early reading and schooling taught him firm values, authority, and a beneficent and yielding world. Lastly, Grant's sense of religious mission followed closely the general pattern. "Innovators in the early stages of growth seem to be characterized by a common ethic which is appropriately termed religious in nature, whatever their religious dogma," Everett Hagan has written. "They feel a personal responsibility to transform the world that far transcends a profit motive."[19]

There was an additional ingredient in the boy's motivation. Hidden behind his brusque self-confidence and compulsion to succeed were the fears and uncertainties of a poor boy proving himself. Anxieties usually push the highly motivated, and for Heber they had begun early. When he was about six, he and his mother were forced to move from the spacious home on Main Street they shared with Jedediah's other wives and children into a widow's cottage. Later the little boy wandered back and wept. Shaking his fist he vowed that someday as a man he would possess the place.[20] In a sense he eventually did—not as a homeowner, but as principal investor and chairman of the Executive Committee of ZCMI, the large department that came to occupy the old Grant homestead. The contrast symbolized much of Grant's business career. He was ever at heart a poor boy reaching uncertainly but determinedly beyond himself.

The comet began its ascent early. On 5 June 1872, when only fifteen and a half years old, Grant found employment as a bookkeeper and policy clerk at H. R. Mann and Company, Insurance Agents. The position had not come by chance. The boy had already prepared himself. Several years earlier he was downtown playing marbles when a lanky young man strolled past. "Do you see that chap there?" asked a companion. "He works in Wells Fargo's Bank and gets $150 a month." Heber's quantitative mind quickly grasped what this meant. He currently was shining shoes at a nickel a pair. To equal the bank clerk's salary, he calculated that he would need more than 240 feet of shoes, six days a week, four weeks a month. He immediately enrolled in a bookkeeping class.[21]

To forego secondary and college education and enter business at an early age was then not uncommon, but Grant had had an attractive vocational option. He refused an appointment to the United States Naval Academy (which would have required considerable remedial schooling) because of his mother's entreaties and perhaps, one suspects, because of an accurate sense of his own limitations.

Heber found his first taste of insurance and financial matters appetizing. He mastered his job easily and quickly. During the day he worked tirelessly. At night he sold policies. Mann and Company occupied the front basement portion of the banking firm, A. W. White and Company, and when duties allowed, Grant volunteered his services at the bank. He offered "to do anything and everything I could to employ my time, never thinking whether I was to be paid for it or not, but having only a desire to work and learn." Mr. Morf, the bookkeeper, in turn schooled his penmanship. Soon Grant's Spencerian hand enabled him often to earn more after office hours writing cards and invitations than he gained from his insurance salary.[22] Three or four years after coming to Mann and Company, Grant assumed the "entire charge of the business," with the exception of writing an occasional letter and actually signing the policies. He bought the company at age nineteen, after Rachel Grant mortgaged her home to provide the necessary $500.[23]

A less confident eye might have seen Grant's purchase as a pig in a poke. H. R. Mann and Company's assets consisted entirely of goodwill, or the inside track in securing policy renewals. In this case goodwill might have no value at all. Would policy holders trust their future business to a nineteen-year-old? Would the national insurance companies transfer their agencies from Mann and Company to Grant? The young man might have customers but no insurance to sell them. Also, there were piranhas waiting to strike. Four other insurance companies in Salt Lake City now commanded the same volume that Mann had once possessed. Agents like the vigorous and clever Hugh Anderson could be expected to attack both Grant's customers and his seven agencies.

Grant quickly proved that he had talent to match his daring. He strengthened his position by forming a partnership, Jennens, Grant and Company, with another Salt Lake insurance agent, B. W. E. Jennens. If Grant required the additional luster of Jennens's maturity and experience, the fast-selling Jennens needed the insurance offered by Mann and Company's agencies. Six of these Grant managed to retain. To help him do so, Hawes and Henry Wadsworth, his former employer at H. R. Mann, actively pulled strings in San Francisco, but Heber's personality also played a key role. When the field representative for one insurance firm arrived to transfer his agency, Grant personally met him at the railroad depot and dissuaded the startled agent from his decision before he was able to lodge at a local hotel. A month and a half after he began business, Grant's correspondence showed a firm hand at the helm. "You think when Mr. Farr returns [to Salt Lake] he will explain the matter to my satisfaction," the adolescent barked when one insurance company attempted to defraud him of a small premium. "The only way the matter can be explained to my satisfaction is to have the draft paid. I shall forward it for collection again and trust it will be honored."[24]

Heber found admiring friends in the Salt Lake business community. "Few young men here are held in higher esteem by all classes than he," the Salt Lake *Herald* wrote in praise of Mr. Grant and his new insurance venture.[25] Prominent bankers Horace S. Eldredge and William S. Hooper signed his insurance bonds. Businessmen Hiram Clawson, W. S. McCornick, and Thomas Webber vouched for his ability and integrity. Webber went further, promising him ZCMI's insurance account. Even the Rev. G. D. B. Miller fell prey to the youth's salesmanship and insured the St. Mark's School. Presiding Bishop Edward

Hunter in turn taught the fledgling a lesson in public relations. The colorful bishop did not care for Grant's initial business advertisement. "H. J. Grant, H. J. Grant, insurance agent, insurance agent," Hunter spoke in his customary staccato echoes. "Who is he? Thought I knew all the Grants, thought I knew all the Grants." When told that H. J. Grant was none other than Heber J., Jedediah's son, he commented in his terse double-speak, "Why don't he say so, why don't he say so? . . . Might mean Helen J., might mean Helen J." When informed of the bishop's views, Grant immediately and permanently changed his business name to "Heber J. Grant."[26]

Buying insurance in nineteenth-century Utah required a personal conversion tantamount to changing one's religion. The industry was only beginning to enter the Utah market, and many hard-line conservatives saw an insurance policy as a violation of family and social responsibility. Besides, Eastern- and European-based companies drained dollars from Utah's colonial economy, a practice despised by LDS leaders. Heber himself could not warm to life insurance for many years. But fire protection made sense, and he had few peers in the marketing of it. For one thing, he sensed the psychological moment to close a deal. The evening after Salt Lake City's destructive 1882 fire, he recorded in his journal: "While standing watching the fireman throwing water on the ruins, [today] I insured L[orenzo] D. and A[lonzo] Young for 5000 and Jos[eph] L. Richards for 5000."[27] His energy was inexhaustible. When he left the office one morning his partner challenged him to make $25 in premiums. "I told him I could make twice that much. I started in at 9 a. m. and talked until after 7 p. m. . . . The total profits for the firm were $101."[28]

He could be equally tenacious in defending a client's claim. When adjusters refused any settlement on the Woolley Brothers' fire in Paris, Idaho, Grant decided to make a personal appeal. "Realizing my inability to fully explain the matter in a letter," he wrote the president of the German-American Assurance, J. F. Downing, "I have decided to visit Erie [Pennsylvania], feeling confident that during a personal interview I can so plainly show to you the unjust and arbitrary manner in which W. Bros were treated."[29] As Grant's train sped eastward, Downing repeatedly wired that he would be out of town and unavailable for an interview. Grant as persistently telegraphed his prospective time of arrival. The two finally met, their strained relations rapidly improved, and German-American eventually paid two-thirds of the contested claim.

However, success with sales and claims did not immediately bring personal prosperity. When Grant married Lucy Stringham on 1 November 1877, over a year since the founding of Jennens and Grant, he stood deeply in debt. The newlyweds therefore spent most of their first year in Rachel Grant's small home. Insurance success, then as now, was a slow accretion, so Heber looked for supplemental income. Jennens, Grant and Company branched out to peddle books. Grant also sought Utah retailers for the Chicago grocery house, Franklin MacVeagh and Company. He briefly considered a brokerage partnership with Richard Young. He did odds and ends for the Deseret National Bank. And he taught penmanship and bookkeeping at the University of Deseret. Teaching gave Grant one of his first opportunities to support home industry. Local merchants had previously refused to sell George Goddard's homemade ink, describing it as inferior. "I know better," Grant remembered telling them, "I am a judge." The professor insisted that his students use the Goddard variety, and the merchants quickly stocked the product to meet the unexpected demand.[30]

However, the most important of these second jobs (it would have occupied almost anyone else full time) was at the Church-owned Zion's Savings and Trust Company. In August 1877, with the vigorous support of the dying Brigham Young himself, Heber was appointed assistant cashier. The position was literally a one-man show: cashier, bookkeeper, paying and receiving teller, after-hours note collector—and janitor. For a young man not quite twenty-one, the selection was impressive, although Grant himself took a different view. "I would not have had the job as a gift," he recalled, "had it not been that it gave me a chance to talk insurance to depositors." His $75-a-month at Zion's was only a third of his other income.[31]

At Zion's Savings, Grant received one of the major shocks of his life. While reading the *Deseret News* one evening he learned for the first time of his "resignation" from the banking concern. Zion's Savings had fired him. The bank board's action probably owed less to Grant's selling of insurance during office hours than to the return of Bernhard H. Schettler from a mission. Schettler had New York banking experience and served as Zion's assistant cashier prior to his proselyting tour. With President Young now deceased, the board apparently felt free to choose the more experienced of the two men. The achievement-oriented Grant was shattered, although he responded, typically, with even greater zeal. "I am half inclined to think that the kicking me out of the Savings Bank was the making of me," he later reflected, "as it started me out to rustle with greater energy than ever before."[32]

Grant's hard work gradually began to pay handsome dividends. A typical Utah wage earner of the time might make annually between $400 and $600. In contrast Grant, still in his early twenties, earned $3,800 in 1878, $5,480 in 1879, and over $6,800 in 1880. He opened another agency in Ogden and dominated Utah insurance. At the same time he began to fulfill his dreams of furthering home industry. Along with Lorenzo W. Richards, he purchased the Ogden Vinegar Works. Grant invested $6,500 of his own earnings and borrowed another $10,000 for the investment.

Grant's steady business climb, however, was not without interruption. On 30 October 1880, just before he turned twenty-four, Grant was appointed president of the Tooele Stake. The new assignment proved enormously difficult and trying. For one thing, Grant's finances deteriorated. His new ecclesiastical duties required much personal time and energy, and his Salt Lake City business declined proportionately. Nor was he able to find any supplemental income in his village home. "I never made a dollar in Tooele during the two years I was president of that stake," Heber recalled, "and my expenses were much greater than they had been before." He was forced for the first time to keep a team and buggy for his official church travel within the stake. There were also the costs of commuting between Tooele and Salt Lake City. Whenever possible Grant spent weekdays in the Utah capital, traveling to and from Tooele on Saturdays and Mondays. In addition he found that as a leading citizen of both communities, he was expected to donate freely in each.[33]

Another far more serious factor in Grant's strained finances involved the Ogden Vinegar Works. The venture was not even meeting costs. By November 1880, Lorenzo Richards had extricated himself from the operation, forcing Grant to incorporate the factory and personally shoulder most of the financial burden. Utahns simply refused to patronize the home-manufactured product. The harried Grant ordered chemical tests on his imported competition and announced that the rival brand was doctored with acetic acid. Still merchants would not push his product. Grant facetiously asked one businessman if he did not wish to purchase Utah Vinegar in two-thirds full barrels, add his own "mineral poison," and make even greater profits. "He thought that would be wrong," Grant recounted, "but he went on selling the stuff manufactured that way. I could not get the patronage."[34]

Then, on 22 April 1881, the vinegar factory burned to the ground, wiping out virtually all of Grant's assets. All that remained were smouldering ruins with a salvage value of several thousand dollars and $9,000 in debts. To add professional embarrassment to his financial distress, the fire insurance salesman found that he was underinsured! The vinegar works, worth between $16,000 and $18,000, was protected by only a $7,000 policy. And it was uncertain whether this insurance was actually in force, for Grant had forgotten to alter the policy's beneficiary from his old partnership to the new corporation. Furthermore he feared the possibility of arson. Had Frank Rother, his manager, intentionally set the fire to conceal his inability to turn a profit? Grant's distress led some to wonder if there might not be a higher meaning in the calamity. Apostle Francis Lyman bluntly told his friend that the fire was a possible heavenly warning to keep his speculations within bounds and to give more prayerful attention to gospel study.[35]

Grant did see a few hints of hope among the dark shadows. Not one of his creditors demanded payment upon his notes.

Three of them actually promised further credit, while James Wrathall of Grantsville began a long relationship with the businessman by lending a large sum. "I found that I had much better credit than I had even expected," Grant exulted.[36] Of course, his creditors were not entirely selfless. By requiring payment they would have invited Grant's bankruptcy, a course which would have given them only a fraction of the cash due them. They, along with Wrathall, were betting their money on Grant's skills and honesty to pay them someday in full.

Moreover, he was able to minimize the disaster at the Ogden Vinegar Works. After seeking Lyman's counsel, he decided to make a clean breast to the insurance carriers. He told the investigating adjustor the full particulars of the improperly assigned beneficiary and was relieved that the companies would pay regardless. Also the plant's manager, Frank Rother, promised several thousand dollars to buy the damaged machinery and real estate.[37]

Nevertheless, for a time Grant's finances remained precarious. Expenses continued to mount and his income continued to decline. He had borrowed to buy his Tooele home only ten days before the Ogden fire. And Rother was failing to make his payments. Grant's friends now suggested that he make an assignment on the vinegar works and throw the disastrous project to the wind. By December 1881, in a desperate attempt to salvage his finances, Grant was working almost every night until midnight and sometimes until 2 a.m. "I would be simply delighted," he often told Lyman, "if . . [the General Authorities] would call me on a mission for ten years, with the privilege after ten years of going back to Salt Lake to be born again, financially speaking, instead of being buried alive out here."[38]

Grant's image of death and burial was more than a passing remark—it evidenced deep distress. He later admitted that during his Tooele Stake presidency he felt so blue that he didn't know what to "do or where to turn."[39] His despair was only partly the result of his desperate finances. He also suffered from the radical change bucolic Tooele had brought to his urban-oriented life. The fact that his insurance and business dealings had not prepared him for his ministry threw him further off balance. And worse, serious illness now entered his home. After only a week in their new Tooele residence, the Grant's second daughter came close to dying. Then Lucy, Heber's wife, began a lingering stomach illness and female disorder that twelve years later claimed her life. These accumulated pressures finally brought Grant himself near to death. His six-foot, 140-pound frame almost yielded to "nervous convulsions," after which an attending doctor solemnly warned if the young man did not slow his pace he should certainly experience a "softening of the brain."[40]

Less than two years after his arrival in Tooele and ten months after his nervous collapse, Grant received a telegram that once more affected his business goals. He was asked to attend a 3:30 p.m. council meeting on 16 October 1882 in President John Taylor's office. Upon arriving he heard Taylor announce a revelation concerning the filling of two vacancies in the Quorum of the Twelve Apostles. As the document was read, Grant learned of his own appointment. At twenty-five he was a member of Mormonism's second-ranking body.

There were whispers and innuendos surrounding his selection to the Twelve. While close associates like Anthony Ivins, Richard Young, Edwin Woolley, Alex Hawes, and Charles Savage, the pioneer photographer, had believed his appointment was only a matter of time, Heber learned it had taken President Taylor's written revelations to convince others that he was apostolic timber.[41] No one doubted his ability or integrity— only his business preoccupation. Grant understood that President George Q. Cannon's prayer of ordination was more than a gentle reminder. "Thou must look upon this calling and this Apostleship," Cannon warned, "as paramount to everything else upon the earth; money, stocks and all kinds of property must fade into insignificance."[42]

Such comments weighed heavily upon Grant, and during the next several months he experienced a dark night of the soul. To friends he acknowledged that perhaps he should place his business ambitions aside. He resolved to follow the noble example of Apostle Erastus Snow, who labored impecuniously in the service of others. He recognized that money had dominated his short career. Nevertheless he insisted that *"never in my life have I seen the time that I was not willing to change my plan of action at the word of command from God's servants."* To prove his point, had he not gone to Tooele at fearful financial sacrifice? And while there, he repeatedly offered to sever his remaining Salt Lake City business ties if his church leaders so desired. *"Cash* has not been my God," he stoutly maintained; "my heart has never been set on it, only to do good with what might come into my possession."[43]

At other moments Grant's abnegation wavered. He wondered whether he could cast himself in the image of Erastus Snow. Must not he be himself? He understood that Apostles of his time were allowed to do considerable private work. He also knew that he had a rare business gift and enjoyed making money. Should he totally ignore his talents and interests? Significantly, Grant occupied in the Quorum of the Twelve the vacated seat of the scholarly Orson Pratt, whose death had left his wives and children impoverished. The new Apostle did not want a similar fate for his own family. He remembered both his childhood poverty and his recent critical illness. Might he be closer to Pratt's example than he realized? Weighing all these factors, Grant set for himself a new goal. Whenever his apostleship permitted, he would work at amassing $100,000. Then, with money in the bank, he would devote all his time to the ministry.[44]

While not personally avaricious, he did confess to a very strong desire for wealth and believed that someday he would have it. Yet he scrupulously insisted upon an accompanying proviso: "Heavenly Father . . . [must] give me wisdom to make a proper and beneficial use of the same." His pet ambition was "to have a lot of money and to have no love for it and to do good with it."[45]

Grant's ideas on beneficial wealth were the Mormon version of the Gospel of Wealth then sweeping America. The Reverend Russel H. Conwell, who delivered his lecture *Acres of Diamonds* some six thousand times, described the viewpoint of the LDS entrepreneur to a tee. "To secure wealth is an honorable ambition, and is one great test of a person's usefulness to others," Conwell asserted.

"Money is power. Every good man and woman ought to strive for power, to do good with it when obtained. Tens of thousands of men and women get rich honestly. But they are often accused by an envious, lazy crowd of unsuccessful persons of being dishonest and oppressive. I say, get rich, get rich! But get money honestly, or it will be a withering curse."[46]

Grant may have first received these doctrines from his exemplar Brigham Young, who preached in a similar vein. But their popularization throughout America at the time Grant launched his career undoubtedly put resolve in his spine. The young man planned to personify the proper uses of wealth.

From his youth he lived simply. Moreover, unlike many tycoons of the era who spent lifetimes accumulating money and their few last years dispensing it, Grant's generosity bloomed early. For example, when the boy-businessman heard Bishop Woolley appeal for donations, he gave $50, despite other pressing demands. At first Woolley demurred, saying it was too much. Grant insisted and paid his money.[47] Even when the debts of his vinegar works pressed upon him, he donated liberally; almost one-fifth of his income in 1881 went to the church and civic projects as well as to the needy.[48]

During the 1880s his gifts to friends and worthy purposes were often twice as great as his tithing—or over 30 percent of his income. Even the liberal-minded Francis Lyman could not fully approve his course. While Lyman believed that the young man should do his full share in aiding others, he wondered if Grant's donations weren't out of proportion to his means. Still Grant continued to give. "I do try to feel another's pain and to aid all that I can to lessen it," he wrote in his journal after a friend had written expressing appreciation for an "anonymous" gift. "He is correct in thinking I aided him. . . . I sent his family $300 by James H. Anderson while he was in the penitentiary [on cohabitation charges] but I requested brother Anderson not to inform them from whom the donations came."[49] Obviously, the scale of Heber's giving made anonymity difficult.

Grant believed his capitalist stewardship involved more than the giving of alms. In the decade following his call he embarked upon what he described as a temporal ministry, using his money and talents to prosper and defend the Saints. First he preached and continued to practice home industry. In sermon after sermon he raised his voice to defend Brigham Young's old battle cry. Nor was he content with mere words. Grant-manufactured and Grant-sold products became familiar Utah items. He himself always tried to wear "homemade." When the Utah assembly feted its Wyoming counterpart, Grant's legislative duties required that he purchase an imported black suit and Prince Albert coat. However, fearful that his continued example might impair the home-industry cause, immediately after the ball he gave the expensive attire to a relative. "I have been called a crank on homemade goods," he admitted, "and I am pleased to have the title."[50]

The second element in his temporal ministry was more combative. During the 1880s Mormonism was pushed to the wall. Anti-Mormons in Utah, who were often merchants, attempted to wrest economic and political control from Church leaders, while congressmen in Washington passed punitive legislation against the Saints. Grant defended the Mormon kingdom by founding "home institutions," businesses that would deprive anti-Mormons of their commercial profits and power. Of course, home industry and home institutions went hand in hand. "I hope to see . . . [home industries] come into general favor not only because they are good and worthy of the support of the people," Grant once explained, "but because the money which is spent for them stops in the country and assists me and others to maintain home institutions and to start others . . . that is the dream of my life in a business line."[51]

The tension between ministry and money continued to agitate Grant for several decades. However, once he came frankly to assess his talents and embark upon his temporal ministry, his self-doubts and melancholy noticeably lifted. Clearly this was not an Apostle in the traditional mold. Other men might speak publicly on theology or see visions and dream dreams. Heber might have similar private experiences, but his

public religion lay in duty, observance, charity, and building the
temporal kingdom. When an anti-Mormon newspaper caustic-
ally suggested that Grant's favorite hymn was "We Thank Thee,
O God, for a P-r-o-f-i-t," the Apostle cheerfully conceded some
truth in the remark.[52] Grant acknowledged that the Church
required men of differing talents. His talent was financial. He
would improve the material well-being of the Saints.

Upon returning to Salt Lake from Tooele in 1882, Grant
appraised his money-making to date. His success had been
moderate at best. "I have had many ups and downs in the past
five years," he wrote his cousin, Anthony W. Ivins. "During the
five years I have made, including $2,000 from Father's Estate,
about $26,000—perhaps $27,000." He actually had little to
show for his income. His assets might have been valued at
$6,000 or $7,000, with most of his cash tied up in the real estate
of the two homes occupied by his mother and his own family.
Grant took consolation for what he described as his poor
showing in knowing that during the period "I have paid a full
tithing; donated liberally to the poor, temples, assembly hall,
missionaries, etc.—and that none of my money has been spent
in gambling, purchasing liquor, [or] tobacco."[53]

Too, he had high hopes for his financial future. In addition
to his yearly General Authority living allowance of $2,000, he
could count on his insurance business annually netting him
$2,500. Since his original partnership with Jennens, Grant had
taken his insurance company through a series of reorganizations. Each had made it more profitable. Furthermore, Grant
had found a new investment. His half brother, B. F. Grant, had
gratuitously given him a half share in his forwarding and
commission business at Milford in southern Utah. This Heber
calculated would bring in another $1,500 and $2,000 a year. "I
see no reason, provided I do not have to give up my
business[es]," he summarized, "why I should not have [saved]
fully $10,000 in hard cash when I am 30 years old."[54] He was
giving himself only four years.

Milford was a railroad terminus that served the wild and
rich Frisco Silver Mining district, less than twenty miles to the

northwest. Grant Brothers wholesaled and plied supplies to the mines. For several months the Milford business seemed a bonanza. Heber received his first intimation that the venture might be flawed when he inspected its books and found that his half-brother had overpaid $500 when buying the concern. The oversight was symptomatic. Within less than a year B. F. Grant was bankrupt and his half-dozen Milford businesses in disarray. From his distant office in Salt Lake City, Heber for several years vainly tried to salvage something. But his new partner in Milford not only failed to collect the business's accounts, to Grant's mortification he also rented part of its premises to a saloon. Finally the Apostle cut short his losses and sold out.

Grant could not have considered the Milford forwarding business more than a commercial skirmish. In January 1844 he launched what actually was his first major commercial venture. Along with Joshua Grant, his brother, and George Odell, his cousin-in-law, Grant purchased the implement business of B. Mattison and formed Grant, Odell and Company. "The special legislation that has been enacted against our people was the cause, as much as anything else which led us to engage in the wagon and machinery business," he later explained. "Prior to the formation of the firm of Grant, Odell and Company, almost the entire control of the wagon and implement business was in the hands of men whose interests were inimical to our people; and in some cases these parties used a portion of the means which they had made from the Mormon people to try to procure special legislation detrimental to their interests."[55] Like a general reconnoitering a battlefield, Grant had surveyed a strategic salient and attacked. Grant, Odell and Company was his first home institution.

The selling of buggies, wagons, and farm machinery in Utah had a shaky history, and Salt Lake City bankers were cautious when Grant asked for financing. The company was forced to turn to private lenders such as James Wrathall of Grantsville and to pay usurious interest. Within a year after its organization, without ample capitalization and financing, Grant, Odell and Company was almost at the end of its financial tether.

Grant would replay the wagon company scenario several

times with other companies: inadequate financing, desperate scrambling to meet obligations, and then triumphant success. Odell proved an able manager, and business from the first was unexpectedly brisk. By April 1885 the partnership was broadened into a corporation. A year later the company was rechristened the Cooperative Wagon and Machine Company, a change Grant believed would improve its public image and marketing. "Human nature is such that many men don't like to see a firm successful but they don't object to a Cooperative Company succeeding."[56] By the end of the 1880s bankers were asking the company to take loans, and the conservative money man James Sharp climbed aboard as a major investor. During its first seven years, the company became the largest wagon and implement dealer in Utah, accumulated $100,000 in reserves, and consistently paid an annual 12 percent dividend. It made Grant's business reputation.

From its beginning the wagon company was a semi-religious venture, a business of the Mormon people. It paid tithing to the Church before issuing dividends. Officials curbed swearing by employees and threatened to dismiss the former mule-skinner B. F. Grant if he didn't desist. One major reason for incorporating was to attract prominent Church leaders as investors. Grant wrote LDS stake presidents offering them stock, reduced his own holdings to allow others to invest, and personally guaranteed against loss stock options for the First Presidency. Such action not only placed profits in the proper hands but enhanced the firm in the eyes of Mormon consumers. "I feel that the . . . men that are now associated together in our firm are much more worthy of the patronage of the Saints than those who are not of us," Grant pointedly wrote to one local bishop. "There has never in my opinion been a time when it was more necessary for me to support our friends only, than now."[57]

The Cooperative Wagon and Machine Company provided Grant an ample field for his salesmanship. But he insisted that there was not religious arm twisting. "I know quite an amount of business naturally comes to me on account of being an Apostle," the young businessman admitted. "This I am willing to accept but nothing that comes because a person feels that he is under any obligations."[58] The anti-Mormon Salt Lake *Tribune* had a more jaundiced eye. "Apostle Heber J. Grant . . . sells wagons and mowing-machines to Saints on the score that he is an Apostle and he will deal by the brethren bètter than any wicked Gentile would," the paper wrote with begrudging admiration. "He sells threshing-machines and horse rakes to Gentiles on the score that he has so great a custom among his own people that he can afford to sell to Gentiles cheaper than any Gentile man or firm can."[59]

In the fall of 1885, only a few months after the wagon and implement company turned solidly into the black, Grant embarked on a still more difficult mission. The pro-LDS Salt Lake *Herald* threatened to suspend publication. Since 1870 the Mormon leadership had informally sponsored the morning newspaper as a foil to the anti-Mormon press. By remaining in private hands, the *Herald* could grapple with its opponents on their own terms while the Church-owned *Deseret News* sedately preached in the evenings. The *Herald* owners estimated that the newspaper required a transfusion of $51,000, which they attempted to raise by issuing new stock. But to subscribe invited future liability, and by the middle of November the campaign for new investment money stalled $16,000 short of the goal.

Grant and other church leaders worked desperately to save the newspaper. The anti-Mormon clamor of the 1880s was reaching tumultuous proportions, and the Kingdom needed a journalistic defender. By 15 November, President John Taylor issued a circulating letter pleading for the Saints to take more stock. Four days later Grant asked the assembled *Herald* subscribers to dig deeper into their pockets, but found no takers. Grant himself was finding sleep difficult. In the early morning of 20 November, he made a personal resolve: "I would either go under with the *Herald* or save it."[60]

With that resolve came a plan of action. Grant offered personally to raise the remaining money if paid $3,000 in *Herald* stock. His first day of soliciting brought $11,200. He had already borrowed heavily to invest in the wagon company but found that by mortgaging his home he could raise $2,000 more. Grant, Odell and Company chipped in another $3,000, and the rest came from men who had refused Grant several days before. "Certainly I have great cause to be thankful to my Heavenly Father for the success of today," he penned in his diary. "Only two persons have refused to increase their subscriptions."[61] Within ninety days he completed his fund raising.

Heber had saved the *Herald*—at least temporarily—but the question remained whether the newspaper would be as kind to its new and now largest stockholder. It had never been consistently profitable. Its owners bought stock out of civic and religious duty and not because of hoped-for profits. Likewise Grant invested to protect the Mormon Kingdom, but his risk was far greater than the others. He had imperiled his own credit and that of his fledgling wagon company. If the newspaper continued to sink, it could take him with it. It is no wonder that several days after Grant decided to intervene personally he was prostrated by nerves. "I had intended to go to North Jordan to preach [today]," he wrote, "but did not consider it wisdom to do so, on account of my extreme nervous condition."[62]

During the late 1880s no business project claimed more of Grant's time than the *Herald*. First as vice-president and later as president, he took charge. Within a year he had installed a new editor and a new business manager, Edward H. Anderson and Horace G. Whitney. Grant himself wrote slashing, off-the-top-of-the-head editorials that surprised his friends for their ability. In 1889 the newspaper adopted a more pleasing format, and a year later it was printed on a new-fangled perfecting press. As profits began to accrue, Grant expanded features and coverage. Within five years the *Herald* was a new journal.

Grant later admitted that he felt "a particular charm" in controlling the newspaper, a privilege he would willingly pay for.[63] But by the end of 1889 that no longer seemed necessary. Reflecting its new management and the territory's booming economy, the *Herald* now repaid what Heber described as immense profits. On 30 December 1889, the firm's directors surprised Grant with a $1,500 bonus. Not only had he secured large advertising increases, he also had netted the newspaper over $3,500 for its special Christmas issue. He had personally authorized an increase for the issue from 10,000 to 25,000 copies—and then sold 13,000 of the papers himself. The price of the *Herald's* stock responded accordingly. From the time Grant assumed control of the newspaper in 1886, its shares rose almost four times in value.[64]

This was prologue to Grant's greatest financial coup. In the first days of March 1887, a month after completing the *Herald* subscription drive, Grant offered to manage the sale of the Church's 3,500 ZCMI shares, worth more than $300,000. Two weeks before, by enacting the draconian Edmunds-Tucker Act, Congress had threatened to seize all Church property in excess of $50,000. LDS leaders scurried to sell holdings before having to turn them over to the government. President Taylor had already tried to market the ZCMI stock, but cautious financiers judged the times perilous and demanded a large drop in the stock's price.

In contrast, Grant ebulliently brushed these doubts aside. His mission was to defend LDS institutions. Besides, he saw a personal financial opportunity. The Edmunds-Tucker turmoil had depressed the price of ZCMI stock, making it an irresistable bargain—even if the price did not drop to levels demanded by the more cautious.

On 10 March 1886, only three days after receiving President Taylor's go-ahead, Grant informed the First Presidency of the Church that he had arranged the sale. He planned to take 500 shares himself and sell the remaining 3,000 to a hastily formed investment syndicate, eventually known as Armstrong, Farnsworth, and Company. The latter was composed of ten Mormon financiers, including Grant and such prominent figures as Francis Armstrong, George Romney, Philo T. Farnsworth, John Murdock, Francis Lyman, and John Henry Smith. Grant refused President Taylor's suggestions that the firm also include Horace Eldredge, James Little, and Jesse Sharp—the most prominent businessmen in the city. The benefits of the purchase, Grant believed, should go to men "with more faith and less money," Mormon Kingdom-builders of his own stripe.[65] The Armstrong, Farnsworth, and Company partners paid a scanty 10 percent down and pooled their credit for five years to meet the remainder of the purchase price.

Hopefully in the interval ZCMI's annual 10 percent dividend would more than meet the loan costs while the stock rose to its actual value.

John Taylor responded warmly to Grant's action. For the first time since his appointment as a General Authority, Grant felt the distance narrow between himself and his leader. Previously Taylor had cautioned Grant for his business mindedness; his manner toward the new Apostle had seemed cold and unappreciating. But during the ZCMI negotiations, the Mormon President cordially placed his arm on Heber's shoulder and praised his dedication to God's Kingdom.[66] Grant never forgot the moment. It was one of those spontaneous, private gestures symbolic of something larger than itself. Grant's religious leader—the man whose opinions he prized most—had come to appreciate his temporal mission. The act seemed to sanction Grant's deepest drives and ambitions.

The late 1880s were kind to Heber Grant and his enterprises. Utah prospered as never before. Its mines enjoyed heavy demand and high prices. The value of Salt Lake City real estate skyrocketed—two, three, and in some cases more than six times their values of a decade earlier, and speculators declared even these prices to be cheap.[67] Credit was readily available. Banks might charge between 7 and 9 percent on loans, but a well-run business might annually return 10 percent on an investment. Reflecting the good times, the flagship of Grant's stock portfolio—ZCMI—navigated a steady upward course. By 1891 the stock was selling at over $140 a share—twice what Grant had paid for it.[68]

With fortune so easily yielding her charms, the young businessman-Apostle worked passionately. New inventions were an irresistible lure (by 1900 he calculated that he had lost $2,000 in buying patents that proved worthless).[69] He bought the Utah rights to make and sell the Little Joker Washing Machine. He marketed Utah Southern Railroad bonds. He considered and then rejected, for a variety of reasons, building a Salt Lake City hotel, purchasing Idaho farm lands, and starting a local jewelry store. Instead he invested in a Salt Lake City mercantile business, Mexican timber lands, the Mountain Summer Resort Company, an Idaho flour mill, beehives in Tooele, a ranch in southern Utah, and Charles W. Nibley's highly profitable Oregon lumber business. He collected director-ships as naturally as Penelope gathered suitors. Zion's Savings and Deseret National, the two main Mormon banks of the 1880s, claimed him as a director. He also served on the board of the *Contributor* (a magazine for young LDS men), Zion's Benefit Building Society (a building and loan institution), the Social Hall Society (Salt Lake City's oldest recreational facility), and the Salt Lake Literary and Scientific Society (a semi-Church holding company with title to such properties as the Council House and the Deseret Museum).

However, these activities were sidelights to Grant's main concerns. He continued to found and maintain home institu-tions. Less than a month following his ZCMI purchases, Grant was asked by his fellow Apostle Wilford Woodruff to arrange "carriages from among our friends" for his wife's funeral cortege.[70] Grant found the request difficult to satisfy. The Salt Lake livery business was tightly controlled by Gentiles with a reputation for anti-Mormon slander. In fact, in the minds of the Mormon leaders, the city's hack drivers were largely responsible for the Church's tarnished public image (along with the editorial writers of the Salt Lake *Tribune* and the proprietors of local hotels).[71] Grant's immediate frustration in securing "friendly carriages" sparked him to action. In April 1886 he organized the Grant Brothers Livery and Transfer Company and began a furious war to control the local cab and transfer business.

The business actually had little to recommend it. Livery profits usually were low, and in Salt Lake City the prospects of a Mormon-owned company were dim. By owning the city's main hotels, the gentiles controlled a principal source of cab and transfer traffic. Predictably, at the outset, Grant Brothers Livery absorbed heavy losses, and after two years Mormon leaders, who had invested $22,500 in church funds in the project, bailed out at eighty cents on the dollar.

But Heber plunged ahead. Grant Brothers Livery advertised vigorously, bought the latest equipage, including the magnificent forty-passenger Raymond Coach, and built the "great West Temple Street stables," boosted in the local press as the largest west of Omaha.[72] By the end of 1888 Grant played his trump card. He dangled ZCMI's profitable freight business before the territory's two competing railroads, the Union Pacific and the Denver and Rio Grande, suggesting ZCMI's contract might depend on Grant Brothers receiving the railroads' local transfer trade. The tactic was decisive. By 1890 Grant had his railroad contracts and Grant Brothers Livery was undisputed master of the terrain.

A flurry of other home ventures followed. In the fall of 1886, Grant organized the Home Fire of Utah and proceeded three years later with the Home Life of Utah. The Apostle hoped that the two insurance companies would plug the drain of insurance premiums from the territory and also provide money for local investment. In 1888, when the 125-man firm needed a transfusion of cash and energy, the Provo Manufacturing Company named Grant a director. The woolen works were the largest producer west of the Mississippi. By 1889 Grant secured control of the majestic but unprofitable Salt Lake Theatre. The Church had built the playhouse twenty-seven years earlier and had retained tacit control through a series of friendly owners. With no one else willing to assume the burden, Grant took control. And in 1890, when he sensed that the two LDS banks inadequately served their Mormon clientele, he founded the largest capitalized bank ($500,000) in the territory, the State Bank of Utah. "There is no business that can aid [home] institutions . . . so much as a bank," he wrote characteristically, "and I think an effort should be made to retain as much as possible all of the business of every class in the hands of our people."[73]

By the end of 1890, Grant's economic kingdom building had won him a remarkable array of titles and powers. As chairman of ZCMI's executive committee, he oversaw the territory's largest wholesale and retail business. In addition he served as president of an insurance agency, a wagon and implement dealership, and a livery stable—each of which dominated their respective fields. He also headed two insurance companies and one of Salt Lake City's largest banks, published the Mormons' most influential newspaper, and owned the city's main recreational attraction. Grant had in fact amassed the $100,000 which he had set out to obtain eight years earlier. His youthful ambitions had not been in vain. At least for the moment, he had climbed the summit of Salt Lake City's commercial mountain.

Notes

1. Quoted in Katherine Drinker Bowen, *Biography: The Craft and the Calling* (Boston: Little, Brown and Company, 1968), p. 145.

2. *New York Weekly Ledger: LDS Conference Reports*, June 1919, p. 119 (hereafter cited as *CR*). For his youthful business dealings: Heber M. Wells, *Improvement Era* 39 (November 1936): 687. On its most common level, the word entrepreneur means "one who assumes the risk and management of business." Such behavioralists as Everett Hagan and David McClelland, as I shall cite later, also use the term to describe a special personality type often found in the world of business. In this essay I intend both meanings.

3. Heber J. Grant (hereafter cited as HJG), *Improvement Era*, 44 (September 1941): 524; HJG Manuscript Diary, 7: 275, 3 August 1886, HJG Papers, Library-Archives of The Church of Jesus Christ of Latter-day Saints, Salt Lake City (hereafter referred to as LDS Archives); HJG to Lucy Grant, 17 April 1890, Lucy Grant Collection, LDS Archives, and HJG to Allie Ford, 6 September 1899, Letterpress Copybook 29: 400, HJG Papers.

4. Quoted in Merle Curti, *The Growth of American Thought* (New York: Harper and Row, 1964), p. 629.

5. HJG to Edward Anderson, 5 and 6 June 1900, Letterpress Copybook, 30: 619-20 and 622, HJG Papers.

6. Joseph Elder: HJG, *Improvement Era*, 1 (April 1898): 395-96. Edwin Woolley: HJG Manuscript Diary, 3: 194, 16 October 1881.

Alex Hawes: HJG, *Improvement Era*, 42 (June 1939): 329; HJG Typed Diary, 20 and 25 August 1887; HJG to Hawes, 28 March and 29 September 1896, Letterpress Copybooks, 6: 662-63 and 23: 345-46; HJG Papers.

7. Orson F. Whitney, *Through Memory's Halls: The Life Story of Orson F. Whitney as Told by Himself* (Independence, Mo.: Zion's Printing and Publishing Co., 1930), p. 43.

8. Ibid., pp. 43, 66-67; HJG to Edward H. Anderson, 5 June 1900, Letterpress Copybook, 30: 621, HJG Papers; and HJG, *Improvement Era, 39 (May 1936): 268.*

9. *CR*, April 1908, p. 56.

10. Fowler: HJG to Allie Ford, 9 June 1895, Letterpress Copybook, 20: 487, HJG Papers. Working in a hurry: HJG to Lucy Grant, 18 April 1892, Lucy Grant Collection. Resignation: HJG, *Improvement Era*, 3 (December 1899): 83; and 43 (March 1940): 137.

11. HJG, *Millennial Star* 93 (19 November 1931): 760; *Improvement Era*, 39 (November 1936): 668; *CR*, October 1921, p. 13; and the Relief Society Minutes of the Thirteenth Ward, Book B: 1898-1906, 13 February 1902, p. 95, LDS Archives.

12. HJG, *Millennial Star* 93 (19 November 1931): 760.

13. HJG to Heber M. Wells, 29 January 1892, Letterpress Copybook, 12: 170-71, HJG Papers. See also HJG to Lucy Grant, 13 March 1883, Lucy Grant Collection.

14. HJG, *Improvement Era*, 39 (May 1936): 267. See also HJG to Rachel Grant, 4 November 1899, Letterpress Copybook, 29: 632, HJG Papers.

15. Quoted by Harold B. Lee, "Qualities of Leadership," an address to the Latter-day Saints Students Association, August 1970 Convention (published privately), p. 6.

16. HJG, *Improvement Era*, 37 (March 1934): 160; and *CR*, April 1900, p. 23 and April 1908, p. 58.

17. Richard W. Young Diary 2: 3, 4 November 1882, Western Americana, Marriott Library, University of Utah, Salt Lake City.

18. *CR*, April 1900, p. 23.

19. Everett E. Hagan, *On the Theory of Social Change* (Homewood, Ill.: Dorsey Press, 1962), p. 93. For data on child-rearing, see particularly David C. McClelland, *The Achieving Society* (Princeton, N. J.: D. Van Nostrand Company, 1961), pp. 356-73, who summarizes at least a dozen studies as well as providing information of his own. For reading and schooling patterns of achievers, see Thomas C. Cochran, "The Entrepreneur in Economic Change," *Explorations in Entrepreneurial History* 3 (Fall 1964): 26. On the urban, middle-class backgrounds of promotors, see F. W. Taussig and C. S. Joslyn, *American Business Leaders: A Study in Social Origins and Social Stratification* (New York: Macmillan Co., 1932) and Frances W. Gregory and Irene D. Neu, "The American Industrial Elite in the 1870s: Their Social Origins," in William Miller, *Men in Business: Essays in the History of Entrepreneurship* (Cambridge, Mass.: Harvard University Press, 1952), pp. 193-211. I am unacquainted with any motivational studies dealing directly with the child-rearing practices of Mormon society, despite the subject's obvious importance. During the nineteenth century, the influence of Mormon fathers no doubt was restricted by involvement in plural marriage, years-long proselyting tours, and local Church leadership. Did their fathers' absence allow children greater opportunities for self-mastery and thus instill motivational drives? Does this in part explain the achievement record of Mormon men and women?

20. HJG, *Improvement Era* 44 (November 1941): 665, et seq.

21. HJG, *Address to the Deseret News Carriers During Their Annual Roundup* (Salt Lake City: n. p., 1921), p. 7. See also HJG, *Improvement Era* 3 (December 1899): 82.

22. HJG, *Improvement Era* 3 (December 1899): 83.

23. HJG to J. B. Hall, 10 June 1876, Letterpress Copybook, 3: 55, HJG Papers. This copybook is the most important source for Grant's early insurance dealings.

24. HJG to T. M. Benedict, 22 July 1876, Letterpress Copybook, 3: 268, HJG Papers.

25. *Salt Lake Herald*, 23 June 1876.

26. HJG to Edward H. Anderson, 9 July 1901, Letterpress Copybook, 31: 667, HJG Papers.

27. HJG Manuscript Diary, 4: 103, 5 January 1882, HJG Papers. The Mormon analogy of converting Utahns to insurance is Grant's. See HJG to W. G. Bickley, 12 April 1890, Letterpress Copybook, 8: 313, HJG Papers.

28. HJG Manuscript Diary, 2: 69-70, 24 June 1881, HJG Papers.

29. HJG to J. F. Downing, 24 July 1885, Letterpress Copybook, 6: 128-29, HJG Papers.

30. *CR*, April 1910, pp. 40-41.

31. HJG, *Improvement Era* 44 (September 1941): 524. See also Heber M. Wells, *Improvement Era* 39 (November 1936): 687.

32. HJG Press Copy Diary, 2: 407, 18 July 1890. See also HJG to Thomas G. Webber, 31 December 1890, Letterpress Copybook, 10: 124, and HJG to George T. Odell, 30 January 1892, ibid. 12: 735-36, all HJG Papers.

33. HJG, *Improvement Era* 44 (April 1941): 203. Later in the century, with Grant himself serving on the committee making the recommendation, stake presidents did receive a small living allowance. The practice was subsequently discontinued.

34. *CR*, April 1910, p. 39.

35. Francis M. Lyman Diary, 25 April 1881, LDS Archives.

36. HJG Manuscript Diary, 2: 27, 22 April 1881, and entries for several days thereafter, HJG Papers.

37. Ibid., 2: 36-38, 29 April 1881.

38. HJG, *Improvement Era* 44 (April 1941): 203, and *CR*, October 1916, p. 31.

39. HJG to B. F. Grant, 21 July 1896, Letterpress Copybook, 23: 77, HJG Papers.

40. HJG to W. H. Harrington, 18 February 1890, ibid., 8: 186. Also HJG to Brown, Craig and Company, 18 December 1890, ibid., 9: 178; HJG Typed Diary, 1 November 1887, HJG Papers; and Lyman Diary, 7, 15, 16, 23 January 1882.

41. Grant himself understood that many did not feel sympathetic to his call, (see HJG to Willard Young, 1 February 1892, Letterpress Copybook, 12: 240, HJG Papers). On another occasion he wrote: "I think I am safe in saying that about half of the Latter-day Saints if not two-thirds of them were simply dumbfounded when I was chosen to be a member of the Apostles." HJG to John C. Cutler, 2 December 1891, ibid., 9: 423. For rumors circulating among his friends prior to his appointment, see Ronald W. Walker, "Young Heber J. Grant and His Call to the Apostleship," *Brigham Young University Studies* 18 (Fall 1977): 121-22.

42. A copy of Cannon's blessing is found in HJG Manuscript Diary, 5: 89-96, 27 November 1882, HJG Papers.

43. HJG to Anthony W. Ivins, 22 October 1882, Letterpress Copybook, 5: 7-10, HJG Papers.

44. HJG Typed Diary, 4 November 1899, HJG Papers.

45. HJG to Anthony W. Ivins, 22 October 1882, Letterpress Copybook, 5: 2, and HJG to B. F. Grant, 18 August 1895, ibid., 21: 64, HJG Papers. See also HJG to Anthony W. Ivins, 29 December 1895, ibid., 22: 27.

46. Quoted in Ralph Henry Gabriel, *The Course of American Democratic Thought* (New York: The Ronald Press Company, 1956), p. 158.

47. Abraham H. Cannon Diary, 18 January 1891, Brigham Young University.

48. HJG Manuscript Diary, 4: 27, 1 November 1881, HJG Papers.

49. Ibid., 7: 269, 3 April 1886. Lyman's caution is found in HJG Typed Diary, 31 January 1887, HJG Papers.

50. HJG to John T. Smellie, 12 January 1895, Letterpress Copybook, 20: 11, HJG Papers. Grant told the story of his short-lived attire several times. See for example *CR*, October 1921, p. 10.

51. HJG to John T. Smellie, 12 January 1895, Letterpress Copybook, 20: 11, HJG Papers.

52. *CR*, October 1907, pp. 24-25.

53. HJG to Anthony W. Ivins, 13 November 1882, Letterpress Copybook, 5: 48, HJG Papers.

54. Ibid., 43-44.

55. HJG to E. H. Valentine, 12 February [1887], ibid., 7: 328.

56. HJG to Joseph F. Smith, 4 June 1884 [1886?], ibid., 6: 485.

57. HJG to Horton D. Haight, 29 May 1885, ibid., 5: 495-96.

58. HJG Manuscript Diary, 8: 27-28, 11-15 January 1888, HJG Papers.

59. *Salt Lake Tribune*, 2 June 1890, p. 4.

60. HJG to Charles L. Anderson, 8 December 1885, Letterpress Copybook, 6: 247-48, HJG Papers.

61. HJG Manuscript Diary, 7: 212-13, 21 November 1885.

62. Ibid., 7: 213, 22 November 1885.

63. HJG to Horace G. Whitney, 21 March 1892, Letterpress Copybook, 13: 66, HJG Papers.

64. Immense profits: HJG to Horace G. Whitney in HJG Typed Diary, 2 January 1900. Christmas issue: HJG Press Copy Diary 2: 242,

30 December 1889. Stock value: HJG to Thomas G. Webber, 19 February 1891, Letterpress Copybook, 10: 371, HJG Papers.

65. HJG Manuscript Diary, 7: 253, 15 March 1886, HJG Papers. Originally the leading partner was Henry Dinwoody, but following a fire in his furniture establishment he retired from the firm. Other partners included William H. Rowe, Charles S. Burton, and Junius F. Wells.

66. Ibid., 7: 254, 15 March 1886.

67. Abraham H. Cannon Diary, 28 February and 6 March 1890; Autobiography of Hezekiah Eastman Hatch, p. 37, typescript, LDS Archives; HJG to Joseph H. Richards, 22 February 1890; HJG to Alfred L. Giles, 26 March 1890; HJG to Anthony W. Ivins, 13 December 1890; and HJG to R. D. Foltz, 28 November 1891; Letterpress Copybooks, 8: 215-16, 287-91, 9: 171-72, 394, all HJG Papers.

68. HJG to Moses Thatcher, 29 April 1886, Letterpress Copybook, 7: 93-94. Immediately after the announcement of the sale, the stock rose $10 to $15 a share, apparently due to the view of financial men that church ownership during the difficult days of the raid had depressed its value. For the stock's 1891 price, see HJG to J. B. Powell, 2 April 1891, ibid., 10: 467, HJG.

69. HJG to David K. Udall, 30 May 1901, ibid., 31: 523. As was Grant's practice when calculating losses, this figure included money that might have been made had his patent investments been conservatively invested elsewhere.

70. HJG Press Copy Diary, 1: 92, 27-31 December 1886, and HJG to Joseph F. Smith, 10 April 1886, Letterpress Copybook, 6: 453.

71. HJG Typed Diary, 12 April 1894, and Abraham H. Cannon Diary, 12 April 1894, LDS Archives.

72. *Deseret Evening News*, 22 October 1894.

73. HJG to Moses Thatcher, 22 February 1890, Letterpress Copybook, 8: 210, HJG Papers.